PRIMARY SCIENCE INVESTIGATIONS

Activities Developing from AT1

Robert Johnsey

SIMON & SCHUSTER
EDUCATION

First published in 1992 in Great Britain by
Simon & Schuster Education
Campus 400
Maylands Avenue
Hemel Hempstead HP2 7EZ

Printed in Hong Kong

British Library Cataloguing in Publication Data
A catalogue record of this book is available from the
British Library.

ISBN 0 7501 0239 X

Edited by John Day
Designed by Jerry Watkiss/Kingsway Advertising
Artwork by Brian Hoskin/Simon Girling & Asssociates;
    pages 38, 39, 40, 41, 44, 45, 50, 51, 54, 55, 60, 61, 78,
    79, 86, 87, 88, 89, 94, 95
    Andre Hrydziuszko/Simon Girling & Associates,
    pages 36, 37, 46, 47, 48, 49, 56, 57, 64, 65, 70, 71, 72,
    73, 74, 75, 82, 83, 90, 91
    Mike Lacey/Simon Girling & Associates, pages 42, 43,
    52, 53, 58, 59, 62, 63, 66, 67, 68, 69, 76, 77, 81, 84, 85, 92, 93
Cover artwork by Jane Hannath
Photographs by Martyn Chillmaid
Typeset by Kelvin Meadows/Kingsway Advertising

Photocopying
Multiple photocopies of the pupil's pages may be only made
without payment or the need to seek specific permisson by the
purchasing schools for use in teaching at these schools.
In all other cases, permission to photocopy and distribute
photocopies of these materials must be sought.

The author and publishers will prosecute any infringement of
copyright law as it affects this work.

Acknowledgements
The author and publishers thank Wynne Harlen for
her kind permission to reproduce several of her
'performance indicators' in the tables on pages 29 to 32

They also warmly thank the pupils of the following
schools for their help in producing the photographs:
Bishops Tachbrook Church of England Combined
School, Leamington Spa, St Bedes Middle School,
Redditch; and Woodrow First School, Redditch.

Contents

▼▼▼▼▼▼▼▼▼▼▼▼▼▼▼▼▼▼▼▼▼▼▼▼▼▼

Life and Living Processes

Materials and Their Properties

Physical Processes

Theme index

▼▼▼▼▼▼▼▼▼▼▼▼▼▼▼▼▼▼▼▼▼▼▼▼▼▼▼▼▼▼▼▼▼▼

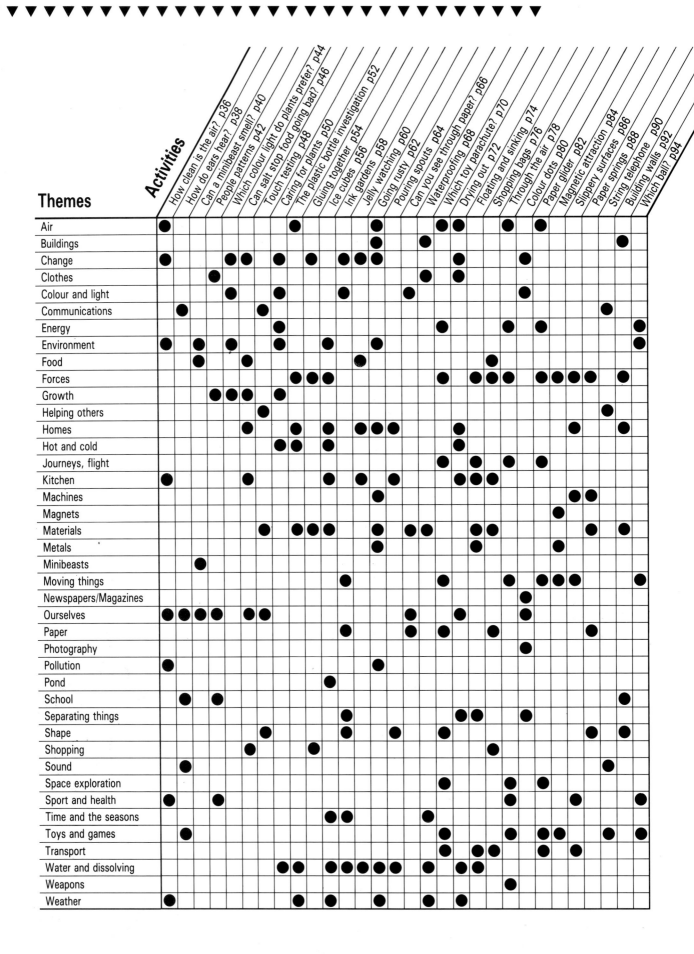

Activities (columns, left→right):
How clean is the air? p36 · How do ears hear? p38 · Can a minibeast smell? p40 · People patterns p42 · Which colour light do plants prefer? p44 · Can salt stop food going bad? p46 · Touch testing p48 · Caring for plants p50 · The plastic bottle investigation p52 · Gluing together p54 · Ice cubes p56 · Ink gardens p58 · Jelly watching p60 · Going rusty p62 · Pouring spouts p64 · Can you see through paper? p66 · Waterproofing p68 · Which toy parachute? p70 · Drying out p72 · Floating and sinking p74 · Shopping bags p76 · Through the air p78 · Colour dots p80 · Paper glider p82 · Magnetic attraction p84 · Slippery surfaces p86 · Paper springs p88 · String telephone p90 · Building walls p92 · Which ball? p94

Themes	p36	p38	p40	p42	p44	p46	p48	p50	p52	p54	p56	p58	p60	p62	p64	p66	p68	p70	p72	p74	p76	p78	p80	p82	p84	p86	p88	p90	p92	p94
Air	●							●				●					●	●			●	●								
Buildings												●		●															●	
Change	●		●	●		●		●		●	●	●											●							
Clothes			●														●													
Colour and light				●	●			●					●		●								●							
Communications		●					●																					●		
Energy						●											●			●			●							●
Environment	●		●		●	●		●			●																			●
Food			●	●		●								●					●											
Forces							●	●	●	●							●	●	●	●	●	●	●	●	●	●	●	●		
Growth			●	●	●			●																						
Helping others							●																				●			
Homes					●			●		●	●	●					●								●			●		
Hot and cold						●	●		●																					
Journeys, flight																	●		●			●		●						
Kitchen	●				●				●			●		●			●	●	●											
Machines												●													●	●				
Magnets																								●						
Materials				●				●	●	●					●	●		●	●								●	●		
Metals												●							●						●					
Minibeasts			●																											
Moving things											●						●					●	●	●	●	●				●
Newspapers/Magazines																					●									
Ourselves	●	●	●	●		●	●								●						●									
Paper										●					●		●		●				●				●			
Photography																					●									
Pollution	●											●																		
Pond								●																						
School			●		●																							●		
Separating things											●							●	●		●									
Shape					●						●			●			●									●	●			
Shopping						●						●									●									
Sound		●																									●			
Space exploration																	●						●	●						
Sport and health	●		●																		●					●				●
Time and the seasons										●	●				●															
Toys and games		●															●						●		●	●		●		●
Transport																	●	●	●	●		●								
Water and dissolving								●	●		●	●	●	●	●	●		●	●											
Weapons																							●							
Weather	●							●			●			●				●	●											

Introduction

▼ ▼

The main purpose of this book is to provide practical examples of the kind of science investigations that can take place in the primary classroom. The process of science (as opposed to the facts and concepts) is described in Attainment Target 1 of *Science in the National Curriculum: 1991* (DES) and will be explored in detail in the following 30 pages as well as in the double-page spreads describing classroom activities (pages 35 to 95). If you prefer to think in terms of concrete examples, you will probably turn to the activity pages now and return to the introductory chapters when you have a taste of what this book is about.

The development of science as a core subject has not been smooth for several reasons. Many teachers have felt, and still do, that their knowledge and understanding of scientific ideas are not sufficient to give them confidence in the classroom. (The kind of science activities required in the primary classroom are not necessarily the same as those remembered from secondary school lessons.) Another major obstacle is the difficulties encountered when organising practical science activities within the confines of the primary classroom, especially if these activities include a degree of open-endedness. A third difficulty lies in

coming to an understanding of the importance placed on the process of science in children's learning and its relationship to scientific knowledge and understanding.

The National Curriculum for science places strong emphasis on scientific investigation and the process of science. Attainment Target 1 and the related Programme of Study clearly state that children should develop an 'understanding of …. procedures of scientific investigation'. At the same time 'The ability to employ procedural understanding is only of value if it uses scientific concepts, however simple, since ideas such as length, force, energy, temperature and electrical current are indispensible elements of the investigations themselves.' *Science: Non-Statutory Guidance* (National Curriculum Council).

This book explores, in very concrete terms, the idea that children should develop their understanding of the world around them by exploring it in a scientific way, building on their own store of scientific facts and concepts.

Children build their own views of the world around them by carrying out scientific investigations.

Making tea

Most people work through a fixed process to make a cup of tea, though there are slight variations on the basic approach.

- Pour water into the kettle.
- Turn on the kettle.
- When the water has boiled, pour a little into the teapot.
- Swish the water around to warm the pot and pour it away.
- Place tea in the pot.
- Re-boil the water and pour into the pot.
- Stir four times.
- Put the lid on the teapot and cover with a tea cosy.
- Wait for about two minutes.
- Put milk in a cup.
- Pour the tea into the cup.

These steps could be described as a *process* for making tea. They consist of a series of skills that are strung together in a sequence. That sequence can be varied in places to give practically the same result: for instance, by pouring the tea into the cup before putting in the milk. Furthermore, each skill, such as pouring boiling water into a pot, could be isolated and practised alone, although it would make more sense to do this in context.

While the tea-making process results in a cup of tea, the science process has a much more powerful function — that is as a tool for exploring and learning about the scientific world. It is, however, made up of a series of process skills that tend to come together in a sequence when carrying out scientific investigations. The process skills are complex and in many instances can be broken down into smaller sub-skills.

Tea testing

John Oakes, who was a keen tea drinker, noticed that some brands produced different strength teas and that these tended to be the more expensive ones. He noticed the similarities in taste between many of the supermarket brands and decided to avoid these in the following investigation.

He decided to ask: 'Which out of Brook Tips and Ty-Bond would make the stronger cup of tea?' His previous experiences gave him a fair idea that 'Brook Tips makes the stronger tea', so he set out to find whether this was true. He realised that he would have to find some way of measuring the strength of different teas and that his test would have to be fair to both brands.

His measurements could involve comparing the strength of colour of the two teas or he might invite his friend Olivia Jones to a tea tasting session.

To be fair to both teas, he would treat them in the same manner by using boiling water and a single teaspoon of tea in each pot. He would make a cup of tea from each pot without milk after letting them stand for exactly one minute.

In the event, Olivia thought that the tea from the white tea pot was the stronger tasting and this turned out to be Ty-Bond, though John Oakes was wise enough not to draw any conclusions from this until he had asked more of his neighbours for their opinions.

John Oakes had approached his investigation in a scientific manner and thus worked through the following process.

OBSERVING	*John Oakes had noticed the differences between various brands of tea.*
ASKING QUESTIONS	*'Which out of Brook Tips and Ty-bond would make the stronger cup of tea?'*
SUGGESTING ANSWERS OR MAKING STATEMENTS THAT CAN BE TESTED (forming hypotheses or making predictions)	*'Brook Tips makes the stronger tea.'*

PLANNING AND EXPERIMENTING

● controlling variables	*These variables were kept the same:*
	  ● *water temperature*
	  ● *amount of tea*
	  ● *time left to stand*
	  ● *method of measuring tea strength*
	  ● *size of teapot*
	This variable was changed:
	  ● *the brand of tea*
	This variable was measured:
	  ● *the strength of the tea*

● measuring − subjectively and objectively ● making observations	*John Oakes employed the subjective views of another person to measure tea strength.*
● repeating measurements to eliminate error	*More people would be asked their opinion before the experiment was complete.*
● selecting suitable aparatus	
● recording results systematically	
● communicating	

ANALYSING RESULTS

● classifying	
● searching for patterns ● making predictions	*Are the more expensive teas stronger?*
● interpreting data	*The results, if based on the colour of the tea, might simply indicate a stronger dye in the tea leaves.*
● making generalised statements	*Teas from a particular part of the world tend to have stronger tastes.*
● using graphs ● communicating	

DRAWING CONCLUSIONS

● communicating these to others	*Ty-Bond seems to be the stronger on the basis of this simple test.*

MAKING MORE OBSERVATIONS AND ASKING FURTHER QUESTIONS	*Would stirring affect the comparative strength of the teas?*

The process skills

▼▼▼▼▼▼▼▼▼▼▼▼▼▼▼▼▼▼▼▼▼▼▼▼▼

The skills of observing, asking questions, planning experiments etc are called process skills. It is not suggested that these skills necessarily form a fixed order in which children should work, although there is a logic in the way one leads on to another. They are often inseparable and readily intermingle in practice, but the teacher will find it helpful to be aware of the process described in this way and may use it as a framework when planning and assessing children's science activities.

Why encourage science process skills?

There are two important answers to this question. The first is that if children learn *how* to find scientific knowledge and understanding and to adopt a scientific approach to forming opinions, then this major skill can be applied to a wide range of situations for the rest of the child's life. It is an adaptable and reliable strategy for dealing with a variety of situations in the future.

The second answer is connected with the current views on how children learn, which have been developed in major research projects such as the Children Learning in Science (CLIS) project at Leeds University and the Science Processes and Concepts Exploration (SPACE) project at Liverpool University and King's College, London. These suggest that children come to school with their very own ideas about the world and how it behaves. Rather than learn new ideas from scratch, children are more likely to build on, modify or completely change the views they already have in the light of their new experiences. They can be encouraged to do this by exploring their own views in a scientific manner. The quality of their science process skills will greatly influence their ability to build new ideas from their old ones. They are much more likely to take note of their own careful observations or controlled experiments than of some casual and perhaps careless activity.

Children should explore their own ideas in a scientific way.

Observing

Observing the world around us is the starting point for most science investigations and it is true to say that without it there would be no science. Observing is about taking in information which in turn leads to asking questions about what has been observed. John Oakes noticed that different brands of tea have different strengths and this led him to investigate further.

A child watching how a snail moves on a leaf might ask: 'Does the snail have hidden feet beneath its body?' To answer this the child might place the snail on a sheet of glass in order to watch its underside as it moves, thus involving further observations.

This example shows that the ability to observe accurately, as well as being at the beginning of scientific activity, is also a skill used to collect data *during* an investigation.

It is important to realise that information can be collected through all the senses and not just the obvious one of sight. Children should be encouraged to feel, smell, listen to and, when it is safe, to taste a variety of stimuli.

A useful activity is based on a set of identical sealed containers such as disused film canisters with perforated lids. A variety of objects can be placed in the canisters to encourage a range of observations to be made. Children might be asked to predict what is in each canister. The canisters should be made to:

- *Feel different (place a lump of Plasticine at one end).*
- *Sound different (half fill one with salt and another with dried lentils).*
- *Smell different (place inside a small piece of cotton wool soaked in perfume or vinegar).*
- *Behave differently when rolled (place some Blu-Tack on the inside wall of the canister so that it rolls with a lurching action).*

Observing how a snail moves may be the starting point for a science investigation.

The sense of smell may be heightened if the sense of sight is removed.

One way of encouraging children to use their senses is to withdraw one or more of them during an activity. Ask the children to identify objects or move around the classroom while blindfolded. Try listening to sounds without seeing the object making the sound. How much harder is it to screw a nut on to a bolt while wearing rubber gloves and perhaps being unable to see it?

Similarities and differences

Any observations are made in the light of previous experiences. We make comparisons and judgements based on what we know already. Faced with a completely unknown object or event, we tend to struggle to liken it to something else in our experience. We will often say things such as 'It sounds like ...', 'It is longer than ...' or 'It looks like ...but it can't be because ...'. This essential comparison with familiar objects, events and measurements is an important feature to encourage when children are observing. They should be asked to note differences between objects and then encouraged towards the more difficult task of finding similarities. It is often quite obvious that two rocks differ in size, colour and texture but to find similarities is often a higher-order skill involving the making of generalisations.

The key to observing effectively

When testing 13-year-olds on their ability to make observations, the Assessment of Performance Unit (APU) found, in many cases, that while pupils had the ability to make relevant observations, they often failed to do so because they could not perceive a reason for it. Dr Anthony Russell (1991) has described how an awareness of the contexts and purposes of observation will help pupils to focus on relevant details. He suggests that: 'The distinctive features of scientific observation are the *purpose* of the observations and the *ideas* or *constructs* (in the observer's mind) used when making them.' If one or both of these elements are absent, then children may not carry out observations effectively.

Focusing attention

A visit to a building site can be a stimulating and at the same time bewildering experience. There is so much going on that there is a danger that important features may be missed. We can help focus children's observation by a variety of means:

- Prepare the children beforehand to look for particular building materials.
- Devise, with the children, a simple questionnaire that they should complete.
- Ask the children to look through card tubes or card 'windows' at certain features. This eliminates much of the excess information.
- Make sketches of certain features.
- Use photography.
- Suggest they make measurements.

Back in the classroom during other activities, some focusing strategies might include:

- Limit the number of items on display at any one time.
- Use a hand lens or microscope.
- Use simplified diagrams which point out the key parts of the thing being observed.
- Use slide presentations.
- Focus on behaviours as well as appearances.
- Suggest measurements are made.

Viewing through a card window can help focus attention.

Observing should not be a passive activity. Children should be encouraged to *do* something about their observations. Responses to observing activities might include:

- Talking
    - to friends
    - to the teacher
    - to a tape recorder.
- Writing a description
    - as prose
    - as poetry
    - as a diary
    - as notes.
- Drawing
    - an accurate likeness
    - a comic strip
    - a series of small details.
- Answering questions
    - from the teacher
    - from friends
    - from a worksheet
    - from a textbook.
- Taking measurements
    - of length
    - of area
    - of volume
    - of mass
    - of force
    - of temperature.
- Classifying objects or sets of observations.
- Taking a photograph, making a video or an audio tape recording.
- Children posing their own questions about the object observed.*
- Making a model likeness or a working model.**

* Children can be encouraged to ask their own questions about an object or a situation and then immediately to answer these for themselves. Questions like these will lead to positive action:

- What colour is it?
- How long is it?
- How many ...?
- What are these parts called?
- What happens if I drop it?
- What happens if I roll it?
- Will it float?
- Will it conduct electricity?

And so on.

Children make observations in greater depth if a working model has to be made, in this case a dandelion parachute.

** The process skill of observing can be enhanced considerably if it is used to provide information for a modelling activity. If the model is to be a working one, such as a magnified copy of a dandelion seed and parachute that has to fall slowly, then accurate observation will be all the more important.

A class of eight-year-old children was asked to make a model of a daffodil flower in as much detail as possible, using the materials they thought most appropriate. As well as their obvious need to observe the real flower head carefully, there was much useful conversation within the classroom about the function of the different parts of the flower they were constructing and the materials they were using to make these.

Progression in observing

It is tempting to think that observing is only concerned with the *appearance* of things but this is only a beginning. The elements in a progression in observing skills might be:

- Looking at the *appearance* of simple objects.
- Observing *other characteristics* of simple objects, such as texture, smell, taste and ability to make sounds.
- Looking at the *appearance* of more complex objects, such as a tree or a person.
- Using *observation aids*, such as lenses, microscopes, video film, photographs, a computer.
- Observing the *behaviour* of simple objects or a set of objects as they move, melt, dissolve…
- Observing more *complex behaviour*, such as the flight of a paper aeroplane or a gerbil in a cage.

Asking questions

There is often an understandable fear amongst some teachers that children, especially while taking part in science activities, will ask questions that a teacher cannot answer. At the same time, there is a general understanding that teachers should encourage children to ask questions and maintain their curiosity in what they are doing. There is no easy answer to this difficulty. Teachers of primary-aged children do need to have a basic knowledge of science so that they can answer such questions as: 'Why does a cycle rider slow down even when the brakes are not on?' But they must realise that even the best qualified teachers of science would have difficulty in answering a question such as: 'What would happen to us if the world stopped spinning?'

An informal brainstorming session will encourage children to ask questions which may lead to further investigations.

In *Progress in Primary Science* (1990), Wynne Harlen suggests that it is often desirable *not* to answer children's questions directly because:

- Giving the answer may prevent the children from finding out for themselves.
- Children may not ask further questions if they cannot understand the answers they get.
- A question may not be what it seems and may not actually require an answer.

She suggests that teachers should learn how to *handle* questions rather than necessarily answer them. To do this successfully, teachers need to recognise different categories of children's questions and learn strategies for turning certain ones into investigations for the children.

Encouraging children's questions

Children can be encouraged in a number of ways to ask questions based on their observations. A group discussion can focus on questions arising from an activity. Brainstorming is a technique which, if used correctly, can elicit a variety of questions. The emphasis here should be on acceptance of all suggestions both fantastic and down-to-earth to enable a greater freedom of thought. Questions thrown up thus can be refined later.

Sometimes a simple device, such as a questions box, can focus attention on the questioning stage. For example, use a 'Wonder

Children should be encouraged to make predictions based on their previous experiences and scientific knowledge.

box' with a posting slit, where each question begins with *I wonder* ... Just giving children time to formulate questions is often sufficient.

Classifying children's questions

Questions that children ask can often be classified by the teacher into different types.

- *Those which are statements not questions.*
  Some birds fly south in winter, don't they?

- *Those asking for simple factual information.*
  What is the name of this insect?

- *Those asking for complex factual information*
  How does a magnet attract an iron nail?

- *Those which might lead to further observations.*
  Why doesn't my paper aeroplane fly straight?

- *Those which might lead to an experiment.*
  Which food does the gerbil like best?

- *Those which might lead to a broad investigation.*
  Why do things float or sink?

In developing science investigations in the classroom, the last three categories of question particularly should be encouraged. These can lead to situations where children construct new or modified ideas through investigation. We cannot assume, however, that children will find it easy to ask questions that might lead to investigations. 'In some cases pupils must have a sufficiently well developed understanding of a concept before they can even begin to formulate the right questions about a problem, let alone solve it.' *(Science: Non-Statutory Guidance)*. This necessary understanding will be developed through a wide range of observing activities and, of course, when a child does ask questions they can be refined and possibly rephrased with the help of the teacher.

Answering questions

Once a set of observations has been made, the questions that arise can be phrased in different ways which, in turn, lead to different kinds of answer. As already suggested, the answer will be a hypothesis or a prediction if its validity is to be tested scientifically.

Making hypotheses or predictions?

In *The Teaching of Science* (1992), Wynne Harlen defines a *hypothesis* as:

> … a statement put forward to attempt to explain some happening or feature.

while her definition of a *prediction* is

> … a statement about what may happen in the future or what will be found that has not so far been found…

For instance, if we ask: 'Why are there so many woodlice under the bricks in the school garden?' the suggested explanation or hypothesis might be: 'Woodlice like squeezing into spaces for safety.' This hypothesis can be tested by carrying out simple experiments. It will be proved either true or false, according to the experimental results – or there may be enough doubt to prompt further experiments.

A prediction is, of course, a look into the future. In contrast to a mere guess, it should be an informed statement based on some previous experience. If the Meterological

Office predicts that tomorrow will be windy with the prospect of rain, the forecast will be based on weather patterns already in progress. If a child predicts that a piece of lead will conduct electricity and thus light a bulb from a battery, this may be based on the child's knowledge that *some metals conduct electricity* and can, of course, be tested scientifically.

These definitions are helpful if we bear in mind these things:

- When we consider an answer to a question that may lead to a science investigation, it can be *either* a prediction *or* a hypothesis.
- Both predictions and hypotheses should be made in the light of some previous knowledge or experience, thus distinguishing them from mere guesses.
- Either a prediction or a hypothesis can be tested for accuracy in a scientific way by employing a 'fair test'.

In our example, John Oakes made a *prediction* that Brook Tips would make the stronger tea, based on his previous observations and knowledge. If the original question had been: 'Why is Brook Tips stronger than Ty Bond?' then his *hypothesis* (explanation) might have been: 'Brook Tips is stronger because the leaves are cut in finer pieces' – again based on his previous knowledge and experience.

Planning and carrying out experiments

The National Curriculum for science suggests that children working towards Level 3 should be introduced to the idea of a 'fair test' and that by Level 5 they should design and carry out 'fair tests' in which the range of measure-ments is carefully chosen. But can we assume children know what a 'fair test' means? Dr Anne Qualter (1991) points out that it is '… important that we do not assume that children know what we mean when we ask them to do a fair test'. In her work with the Assessment of Performance Unit (APU), she found a number of instances in which children did not use fair testing despite the fact that they possessed the skills to do so. This view is supported by Rae Stark (1991) in a report on the Scottish

Children need experience of carrying out a wide range of scientific tests.

A child may be playing informally with some wind-up toys on the classroom carpet. She may quickly 'try out' the effect of making the toy move on to a thin book and then on to a sloping book. The child is saying: 'I wonder what will happen to the movement if it is on a book rather than the carpet.' A mini-experiment is carried out, the effects observed and probably, without communicating or recording anything, the child begins another mini-experiment with the sloping book. A formal experiment may come later from these early observations, with greater control over the variables involved.

A child may carry out a series of short, unrecorded scientific experiments while playing with a toy.

Assessment of Achievement Programme (AAP). He concludes that children's '...variation in attempt and success rates ... of the ("fair testing") tasks indicates that the specific content of the task does have an influence on performance.' It may be that we need to provide children with experiences of testing within a broad range of contexts in order that they can build a clear concept of a 'fair test'.

How long do tests take?

Experiments or 'fair tests' may form the major part of an investigation, such as finding the wash powder which washes the best, or they may take a short space of time when a child 'tries something out'.

Variables

A variable is a quantity that has potential to change during an experiment. When John Oakes made his tea test, he could have used water at different temperatures to make the tea, different quantities of tea in each pot or allowed the pots to stand for different lengths of time. This would have been unfair, so these variables had to be kept the same or controlled. He did, however, change the brand of tea — called the *independent variable* — and had to measure the strength of each cup of tea — called the *dependent variable*. At the end of his test, he could be sure that the strength of the resulting cup of tea was entirely dependent on the brand used and nothing else.

Planning experiments

A number of key decisions must be made when planning an experiment:

- Which *variables* are involved and which ones need to be controlled or kept the same?
- Which *variable* is going to be changed?
- Which *variable* is going to be measured?
- How will *measurements* be made — either subjectively or objectively?

Children should be given the opportunity to choose from a range of measuring apparatus.

- Which *equipment* is best?
- How many times should the test be *repeated* so that reliably consistent results are obtained?
- How should the results be *recorded* and *communicated* to others?

Making measurements

Children will need help in deciding how to measure variables in their experiments. Less experienced children will often rely on a subjective assessment of their results, but as they gain experience they should be encouraged to give a 'score' to or make an objective measurement of the various competing elements.

A group of children wanted to find who, in the class, had the best eyesight, so they devised a chart of coloured shapes for the members of the class to look at. In their minds, the subjects would be able either to see the shapes or not! They needed help in understanding that if they could provide a 'score' for each child, then they could be placed in some form of order. They revised their chart so that the shapes got fainter and fainter and placed score numbers alongside the shapes.

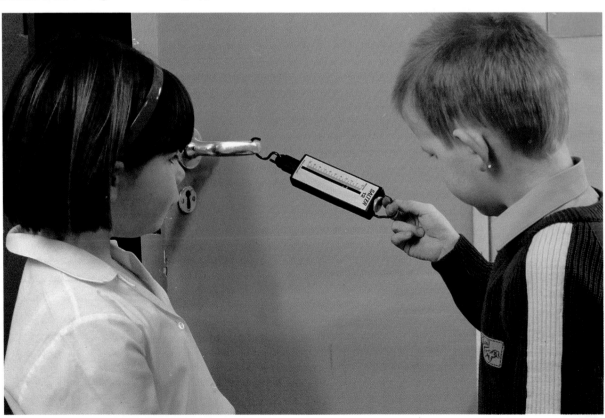

Sometimes deciding exactly what to measure can be difficult. In an experiment to find the effect of using a fertiliser on cress seeds, which is the best variable to measure – height, greenness, taste, speed of growth, size of leaves?

Choosing measuring instruments

Choosing the most appropriate measuring instruments is an important skill which children will not have the chance to practise if they are always supplied with equipment by the teacher. To measure the length of a leaf, a rule graduated in millimetres is required, while a metre stick would be appropriate for measuring out a track for a balloon-powered vehicle. Older children will need to differentiate between using a force-meter which measures up to 10 newtons and one which measures up to 50 newtons when, for instance, they are measuring the force needed to swing open a door. In this case, the 50 newton meter would probably not be sensitive enough (although it would give a measure of the force used).

Repeating tests or measurements

Where possible, children should be encouraged to repeat a test or a measurement a number of times. They should understand that this will help to eliminate the freak result and build up a truer picture of what is going on. This may introduce the problem of finding averages before children have sufficient mathematical knowledge to cope with this. There is no point in children using calculators unless they understand the concept of averages, so this is not always a satisfactory answer. Sometimes the results can simply be added up to form an overall 'score' but again this is not always appropriate. If the number of results is relatively small, say four or five, then it is possible for children to look at their results subjectively to find an approximate average.

Recording and analysing results

The systematic recording of results during an investigation is important because, in the excitement of discovery, facts and figures are easily forgotten! Experimental results can involve words or numbers which could be stored in charts and tables. These will, at first, be drawn for the children but can later be designed by the children themselves.

In the same way that we wouldn't make a cup of tea and then omit to drink it (unless it were the end of break!), it doesn't make sense to carry out an experiment and then omit to search for the answer to the question we asked in the first place. It can too often be the case in school science, however, that the results are not analysed and conclusions are not drawn.

The analysis of results may involve:
- Classifying the data.
- Searching for patterns.
- Interpreting the data.
- Predicting future events.
- Making generalised statements.
- Providing an answer to the original question.

This may be achieved by sorting and/or searching through the results, the use of graphs and pie charts and sharing opinions with others.

Searching for patterns and making predictions

A pattern is the result of something being repeated. If we can work out how the repetitions are arranged, we can use this to predict what comes next or what happened before. Patterns in scientific results can be mathematical, graphic or in some other form. They can often be spotted more easily if the data is ranked in various orders or classified into a variety of categories.

Some children were investigating the behaviour of a single woodlouse when placed in a round dish with a transparent lid on. They traced the paths of a number of different woodlice for one minute each time. When the group placed their diagrams together they noticed that, in most cases, each woodlouse had kept to the edges of the dish and never wandered across the middle. They decided to see whether this pattern was continued when a small obstacle was placed at different locations in the dish.

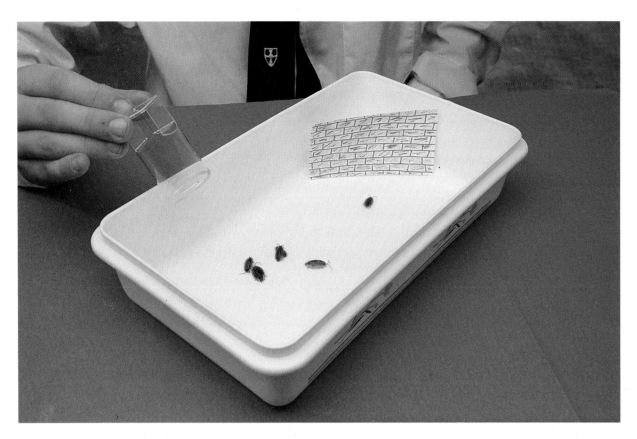

Woodlice are suitable for simple behavioural experiments in the classroom.

Another group of eight-year-old children carried out a survey of opinions amongst their friends involving 20 different brands of crisp. When analysing their results, they noticed a pattern when the crisps were sorted into order of taste. To their surprise, there was a trend towards plain crisps being near the top of the list, and salt and vinegar near the bottom. They predicted, however, that if a similar survey had been done amongst adults, salt and vinegar would have been more popular (because adults often prefer sharper tastes).

A group of children were looking at the results of a simple test to see which eye, left or right, was stronger for each child in the class. They classified the results into various categories and were intrigued to find that left-handed children were largely 'left eyed'.

The search for patterns in data presented as graphs is an area yet to be fully developed in primary science. The use of the computer to support science activities may accelerate this process because of its ability to supply a rapid selection of graphed material on screen. More is said on this subject in the section on information technology (page 23).

Interpreting data

The results of scientific investigations can often be interpreted in a variety of ways. Children's interpretations are usually most fruitful when made in discussion with others. They will find it useful to refer back to the question that prompted the investigation.

Making generalised statements and the nature of science

As a result of their observations and interpretation of results, children may be in a position to make some generalised statements about what they have found. Examples of such statements are:

- All metals conduct electricity.
- Minibeasts will usually move around the edges of the container they are in.
- Children like plain crisps best.
- Magnets do not attract pieces of aluminium.

The statements may or may not reflect the generally accepted view of science knowledge. In fact, these generalisations, which are developed as a result of a science investigation or series of investigations, are *hypotheses* or *general theories* which should be tested over and over again until they are *disproved*. (They can never be *proved* since there may be an exception to the rule waiting round the corner!)

For a long time, people held on to the theory that the world was flat until there was enough evidence to prove this to be untrue. Our current theory is that the world is near spherical and this will stand as a useful model until it is proved untrue. Which brings us to an understanding that science is, in fact, not a body of fixed, irrefutable knowledge – more a set of theories and hypotheses which best fit the facts as we know them and which we are holding on to until they are proved false by further observation and experiment.

Drawing conclusions and communicating these to others

It is at this stage that children reflect on their activity and try to describe and explain what they have learnt. This process of summarising their experiences should help them towards a clearer understanding of what they have done

and the building of their own modified or completely changed scientific ideas. This is often best done in discussion with others in a group or with the teacher before any formal recording is done. Conclusions will have been forming as they worked through their activity, especially when they came to analyse their findings. It may be helpful if they refer to the question they first started with and try to provide an answer to this.

Children can record their ideas in a variety of ways. An oral presentation by a group is often effective and this can be further enhanced by the addition of questions from the class. Children may be able to use their scientific findings to inform a class debate, thus making the knowledge gained more meaningful.

Summarising their experiences will help children towards a clearer understanding of what they have done.

A tape recorder can be used effectively to record a report in the form of a mock radio broadcast, or a new dimension can be added by using video. Children can write their conclusions in a variety of forms, including a newspaper article, a letter or even a dialogue between a child and a sympathetic listener.

Children may be able to mount a display of their work in the classroom and may choose to communicate their ideas through posters and notices. Children's conclusions will include the evidence they have collected during their work, such as tables of data, graphs, diagrams and pictures, as well as some of the artefacts they have been working with. These can all be displayed to good effect.

If children are to develop their scientific thinking at this stage, collaborative work will be especially effective. This can often be achieved by children working with a wordprocessor and sharing the text on screen. This idea is developed further in the section on information technology.

Process skills in the National Curriculum

▼▼▼▼▼▼▼▼▼▼▼▼▼▼▼▼▼▼▼▼▼▼▼▼▼

The National Curriculum in science was the first to be produced. Since then, the original draft provisions have undergone changes in the light of experience and much debate. What has remained constant, however, is the prominent part played by the process of science. When teachers plan schemes of work at Key Stages 1 and 2, up to half of the children's time should involve Attainment Target 1: Scientific investigation. All the elements of the process of science which have so far been discussed in this book appear in a paragraph which has hardly been changed in subsequent updates of the original draft document.

At first measurements may include non-standard measures.

Attainment Target 1: Scientific investigation

Pupils should develop intellectual and practical skills which will allow them to explore and investigate the world of science and develop a fuller understanding of scientific phenomena, the nature of theories explaining these, and the procedures of scientific exploration and investigation. This should take place through activities that require a progressively more systematic and quantified approach which develops and draws upon an increasing knowledge and understanding of science. The activities should encourage the ability to plan and carry out investigations in which pupils:

- *ask questions, predict and hypothesise*
- *observe, measure and manipulate variables*
- *interpret their results and evaluate scientific evidence.*

Science in the National Curriculum (1991).

The key messages about scientific investigation coming from all the reports are:

- Scientific investigations should encourage children to both *use* and *develop* their scientific knowledge and understanding.

- Children should gain first-hand experience of observing and classifying materials and this can be expanded at Key Stage 2 to include the use of secondary sources.

- At Key Stage 2, children should begin to make predictions and formulate their own hypotheses based on their prior scientific knowledge and understanding.

- Measurements may, at first, include non-standard as well as standard measures and will involve increasing precision as the child develops.

- Children will begin carrying out tests that require qualitative measurement but will progress to using more quantitative measurements.

- Children should be introduced to the idea of a fair test at Key Stage 1 and will develop their ideas about controlling variables in an experiment as they move into Key Stage 2.

- Children should be fully involved in recording and interpreting the results of their experiments, searching for patterns when appropriate.

Using information technology to support science activities

▼▼▼▼▼▼▼▼▼▼▼▼▼▼▼▼▼▼▼▼▼▼▼

Information technology is not a curriculum subject − it is tool to be used, when appropriate, to support all curriculum activities. Its potential impact on education has meant that it has been given a special place inside one of the National Curriculum documents *(Technology)* but its sphere of influence should be much greater than this one subject area. Equally, we should not be misled by the high cost of providing software and hardware. There tends to be an aura around things that are costly but this should not suggest that information technology is necessarily the answer.

The humble electric kettle is simply a tool used in the process of, for example, making a cup of tea and in some ways its use can be likened to that of information technology in education. A kettle runs on electricity and may come with an instruction manual to guide us in its use. It can be used for a variety of tasks, such as making tea, preparing gravy or steaming open envelopes. But not all cooking or steaming is done with the kettle! In the same way, we should use IT when it truly enhances the learning process, though this will not necessarily be so on every occasion.

Just as we might give a child instruction in the safe use of a kettle and talk about the variety of jobs it can do, we might instruct children in the uses of a computer or other IT devices. Ultimately, however, we would want the child to decide when and how IT might enhance his or her work. In the future, it may simply be available for use (probably as a laptop computer) in the store cupboard − just as scissors and pencil crayons are today.

Data logging with a computer enhances and extends children's science experiences.

Information technology in the National Curriculum

Attainment Target 5 in *Technology in the National Curriculum* describes how information technology capability can be divided into five strands:

- Communicating: using wordprocessors, graphics programs.
- Data handling: using databases, CD ROM.
- Measurement and control: data-logging and control technology.
- Modelling: using spreadsheets, simulations and adventure games.
- Applications and effects: when is it appropriate to use IT?

Some of the applications in these strands are more appropriate to primary science investigations than others. In some cases, a traditional science activity, such as collecting statistical information about the children in the class, can be extended, by the appropriate use of a database, to store and sort the information. At other times, an IT application will enable children to investigate things that were impossible before the introduction of the computer. For instance, a group of children wanting to monitor the number of pupils entering and leaving a classroom during a whole day can now set up data-logging equipment to do this. They can also keep a constant check on temperature (for instance, inside a wet glove) and watch a graph of the readings develop on a screen as an experiment progresses.

Data handling

Experimental data can be handled in a variety of ways on a computer − from using simple sorting programs to employing complex spreadsheets. A major part of the process of science is the analysis and interpretation of data collected during an investigation. One of the most useful applications is the database with its ability to sort, search and graph data.

Data handling programs can be used to:

- Sort objects into categories and thus form a simple indentification key.
- Store a catalogue of information that can be readily accessed by using keywords.
- Provide a secondary source of information as a 'reference book'.
- Sort data into numerical or alphabetical order.
- Search out a category of information.
- Provide block graphs and pie charts.
- Search for correlations in data using scatter graphs.
- Provide frequency (count) graphs.
- Help in searching out patterns, such as a normal distribution or optimum conditions.

Some children were investigating the way a simple paper aeroplane flies. At first they were intrigued by the way their models flew and spent some time exploring different ways of launching them. They decided to find out which features of an aeroplane design would enable it to fly the furthest.

A wide selection of paper models was made and tested in a fairly random way by different groups in the class. Such data was collected as:
wing length
wing width
distance from tail to nose
number of paper clips on the nose
type of paper used
distance flown by model

The information was collected for 46 different models and was entered on a computer database. The children had been thinking of a number of questions as they carried out their investigations:

- *How does the length of the model affect its flight?*
- *Is tissue paper generally better than sugar paper (or is it too floppy)?*
- *Can the model be too large or too small?*

They were able to sort the results into a rank order with the longest flight first. This showed a writing-paper model with broad wings was the best, but there were so many other factors affecting the flight that some children were not satisfied with this simple result. They were able to search the results to find just the models made from sugar paper and then to sort these into order. The database enabled them to make a wide range of graphs of their results. In particular, a set of scatter graphs showed how one feature, such as wing length, affected flight distance. The scatter graphs were able to show a trend in the results for all the models and enabled the children to predict the features of the ideal model.

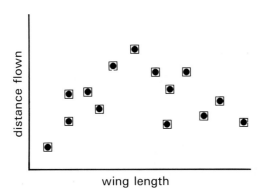

The speed and ease with which a computer database can manipulate information means that children can sift through a wide range of data to find patterns and trends. This is especially helpful and effective when data has been collected by a number of groups within one class and the results are pooled for entry to the computer database. Minor measuring errors can often be smoothed out by the use of a scatter graph (which focuses on trends in results) and, if necessary, corrected easily by returning to the practical activity and taking the measurement again.

Controlling variables

The variables involved in the paper aeroplane investigation could have been controlled at the initial experimenting stage, for example, by varying only the wing length and keeping all else the same. In the example described, however, the variables were 'controlled' by using the searching facility on the database. This can be done by searching out and isolating all the models made from the same materials, with the same wing length and nose weight but with different wing widths. Of course, once the database has been interrogated in this way, more controlled practical experiments can be carried out in the light of the analyses made.

Data logging

Taking and recording measurements are at the heart of scientific investigations, occuring both at the observing stages and during a controlled experiment. Data logging provides the means by which children can automatically monitor and record measurements by electronic means. Sensors, such as those for temperature, light, sound and degree of turn, can be connected to a computer or a remote sensing device to record information even when children are not present. The number of times a switch is turned on or off, or the time taken for an event can be monitored in this way. Suitable software and curriculum support materials are now widely available to primary schools and waiting to be exploited in new and exciting ways.

Wordprocessing and desk-top publishing

Using a wordprocessor to support science activities involves more than simply creating a neatly typewritten report at the end. A word-processor can be employed as a diary which is continually updated as an experiment progresses. The notes can then be edited into a coherent report at a later date.

A wordprocessor is an excellent tool for collaborative writing, whereby children can genuinely share the writing produced on a screen. Many of children's science ideas are best developed through discussion with others either during or after an activity. The need to put their thoughts into writing will add a special focus to the children's developing ideas.

Desk-top publishing packages allow text and graphics to be arranged together on the same page. This will have distinct advantages to those either planning science investigations or reporting their outcomes. The use of a magazine or newspaper approach to reporting science can provide an added stimulus to such work.

Spreadsheets

Spreadsheets are similar to databases in that they can hold information in what can be thought of as a table of rows and columns. One major difference is that the numerical information in one part of the spreadsheet can be related to that in another part by a mathematical formula. A second difference is that if the information in one part of the spreadsheet is changed, related information in other parts will be changed automatically by the computer. For this reason, the spreadsheet is often described as a modelling tool.

Finding averages

The ability of a spreadsheet to calculate values in a certain column makes it a suitable tool when a number of measurements taken in an investigation have to be averaged. The results can be entered on the spreadsheet and the average automatically entered in the appropriate column. The graphing facilities of the spreadsheet can then be used to display relevant data.

More applications

There are other computer applications that have some relevance to primary science investigations, such as simple graphing programs, simulations of science-related events, adventure games and control technology.

Graphing programs may allow simple data to be entered and graphed as a block graph or pie chart. There may be a facility which sorts the data if needed. This kind of software tends to be very simple and therefore limited in its potential but is especially suited to those working at Key Stage 1.

Simulations have their place in the primary classroom but not at the expense of real practical experiences. There is some merit in using a simulation of the growth of a plant, for instance, once children have a broad experience of growing things themselves. The use of the simulation will allow them to hypothesise, predict and experiment with features that might otherwise be impossible or take a very long time.

Adventure games may be based on fantasy or include real-life simulations. They can be used effectively as an initial stimulus for investigations in the real world in much the same way that a teacher might use a book, video or poster to prompt an investigation.

Control technology is an exciting development within primary classrooms. There are many challenges for children and various ways in which they will learn from such activities. Children will develop the technological skills of planning, making and evaluating. They will employ the scientific skills of hypothesising, predicting and experimenting. Children's knowledge of how mechanisms work and energy is controlled can be used in problem-solving situations. Recent developments in which data-logging sensors can be used to control models have forged even stronger links between science and technology activities in the classroom.

Assessment

▼▼▼▼▼▼▼▼▼▼▼▼▼▼▼▼▼▼▼▼▼▼▼

Assessment of children's science process skills is difficult. This book is not the place to discuss all the implications of doing so. One difficulty lies in not having a clear picture of exactly what should be assessed within the complex set of actions that we call primary science investigations. This short introduction to and analysis of the Statements of Attainment for Attainment Target 1 by means of performance indicators is an attempt to clarify the picture.

Teachers have always assessed children's understanding both formally and, more often, informally as part of their overall teaching strategy. For instance, a discussion with a group of children before a learning activity takes place will provide information about the children's previous knowledge and indicate how the teacher should introduce new ideas. More systematic, formative assessment is a difficult but essential task that has, as one of its prime objectives, the ability to inform more effectively the way we teach.

Furthermore, '...the real power of criterion-referenced assessment [is in] revealing to the learner exactly what the expectations are as defined by the criteria; rather than relating achievement to the hidden standards associated with norm-referencing' (Anne Qualter et al, 1990). In other words, children will learn more effectively if the teacher can clearly define for them the targets towards which they are aiming. In the case of teaching factual knowledge, this has been a relatively simple task, while defining the elements of a process is more of a challenge.

The process skills described so far can be broken down into smaller sub-skills, some of which are described in Wynne Harlen's book *The Teaching of Science* (1992). Many of these are included in the table oppposite, which relates the Statements of Attainment for AT 1 to the more helpful 'performance indicators'. Of course, if we want to look for indications that a child can manage a particular skill, then we must provide opportunities for it to be displayed in the activity provided. Thus it is essential that teachers build assessment into their plans for children's science activities.

Teachers might like to adapt the information in the table when assessing children while they carry out the activities in this book.

If a particular ability in science is to be assessed, then teachers must plan activities for children that provide opportunities for the display of such abilities.

Planning for assessment: an example

A teacher planning an investigational activity for a group of Year 4 children might make these decisions:

Theme	Transport
Science investigation	Flying things
Activity	Paper glider - page 82
Assessment	Blue Group (four children working towards NC Level 4)

Science process skills
Answering questions by predicting.

Statement of Attainment
Level 4. Make predictions based on some relevant prior knowledge, in a form that can be investigated.

Performance indicator
Making use of evidence from past or present experience in stating what might happen.

How observations will be made
When the children have made their paper glider and tried it out, they will be asked to pose questions about its flight. Using the most appropriate of these questions, they will be asked to say what they think will happen if changes are made to the design of the glider. Evidence of their using any previous experiences to make these predictions will be noted down.

Notice in this example that:

- The teacher has planned her assessment as part of her teaching strategy.
- The assessment is only for a small, manageable number of children.
- The assessment is concerned with only one part of one Statement of Attainment (that is, using one performance indicator).
- The teacher will rely on direct observation, including questioning of the children.
- The teacher is quite clear how she will *know* if the each child has fulfilled the necessary criteria.
- The evidence collected will be in the form of notes made during the observation.

With similar planning for other groups, the teacher may find time to assess other activities or assess other groups of a similar ability on the same criteria.

OBSERVING

Statement of Attainment	Performance indicators Children will be:
Level 1 Observe familiar materials and events.	While observing familiar materials and events: • making use of several senses • noticing relevant details of the object and its surroundings • identifying differences between objects and events • identifying similarities between objects and events • grouping materials or events etc as a result of observations • discerning the order in which events take place
Level 2 Make a series of related observation.	While making a series of related observations: • making use of several senses • noticing relevant details of the object and its surroundings • identifying differences between objects and events • identifying similarities between objects and events • classifying materials or events etc as a result of observations • discerning the order in which events take place • observing changes over time • using non-standard measures

Level 3
Observe closely and quantify by using appropriate instruments.
	While quantifying observations using appropriate instruments:
	• making use of several senses
	• noticing relevant details of the object and its surroundings
	• identifying differences between objects and events
	• identifying similarities between objects and events
	• classifying materials or events etc as a result of observations
	• discerning the order in which events take place
	• observing changes over time
	• supporting these observations by taking measurements with appropriate instruments such as:
	  ☐ hand lens ☐ masses
	  ☐ ruler ☐ measuring jug or cylinder
	  ☐ weighing scales ☐ thermometer
	  ☐ spring balance ☐ data-logging equipment

Levels 4 and 5	As above but with increasing accuracy and a wider range of instruments such as:
	  ☐ force meter
	  ☐ microscope

ASKING QUESTIONS

Statement of Attainment	Performance indicators Children will be:
Level 2 Ask questions such as 'How ...?' 'Why ...?' 'What will happen if...?' Suggest ideas and make predictions.	• showing some curiosity but without asking questions • asking simple, single questions requiring factual information • asking questions such as 'How ..?' 'Why ...?' 'What will happen if...?' • asking another question as a result of the answer to a previous one
Level 3 Recognise testable questions and ideas.	
Level 4 Ask questions, suggest ideas... in a form which can be investigated.	• asking questions which can be answered by further investigation • being able to re-phrase a question to make it suitable for investigation

ANSWERING QUESTIONS BY: *FORMING HYPOTHESES*

Statement of Attainment	Performance indicators Children will be:
Level 3 Distinguish between a description of what they observed and a simple explanation of how and why it happened.	While making this distinction: • suggesting an explanation which is consistent with evidence • realising that there can be more than one possible explanation of an event or phenomenon
Level 5 Formulate hypotheses where the causal link is based on scientific knowledge, understanding or theory.	While formulating a hypothesis: • suggesting an explanation which is consistent with evidence • suggesting an explanation which is consistent with some scientific principle or concept • applying previous knowledge in attempting an explanation • realising that there can be more than one possible explanation of an event or phenomenon

ANSWERING QUESTIONS BY: *MAKING PREDICTIONS*

Statement of Attainment

Performance indicators
Children will be:

Level 3
Recognise testable... predictions.

Level 4
...make predictions...in a form
which can be investigated.

- distinguishing a prediction from a guess
- making use of evidence from past or present experience in stating what may happen
- explicitly using pattern in evidence to extrapolate or interpolate
- justifying a statement about what will happen or be found in terms of present evidence or past experience

PLANNING AND CARRYING OUT EXPERIMENTS

Statement of Attainment

Performance indicators
Children will be:

Level 4
Carry out a fair test in which
they select and use appropriate
instruments to measure
quantities such as volume and
temperature.

- deciding which variable is to be changed (independent) and which variables are to be kept the same (controlled)
- carrying out the manipulation of the variable so that the investigation is fair
- identifying which variable is to be measured or compared (dependent variable)
- making measurements of or comparisons with the dependent variable using appropriate instruments
- working with an appropriate degree of precision

Level 5
Design and carry out a fair test
in which the range of each
variable involved is chosen to
produce *meaningful results*.

- deciding which variable is to be changed (independent) and which variables are to be kept the same (controlled)
- carrying out the manipulation of the variable so that the investigation is fair
- identifying which variable is to be measured or compared (dependent variable)
- making measurements of or comparisons with the dependent variable using appropriate instruments
- working with an appropriate degree of precision

Statement of Attainment

Performance indicators
Children will be:

Level 2
Use their observations to support conclusions and compare what they have observed with what they expected.

In the light of observation made:
- putting various pieces of information together to make some statement of their combined meaning
- using appropriate graphing techniques
- talking, listening or writing to sort out ideas and clarify meaning

Level 3
Recognise that their conclusions may not be valid unless a fair test has been carried out.

In the light of a fair test:
- putting various pieces of information together to make some statement of their combined meaning
- using appropriate graphing techniques
- talking, listening or writing to sort out ideas and clarify meaning

Level 4
Draw conclusions which link patterns in observations or results to the original question, prediction or idea.

In linking these patterns:
- finding patterns or trends in observations or results of investigations
- identifying an association between one variable and another
- making notes of observations in the course of an investigation
- using graphs, charts and tables to convey information
- choosing an appropriate means of communication that is understandable to others
- using secondary sources of information

Level 5
Evaluate the validity of their conclusions by considering different interpretations of their experimental evidence.

In considering different interpretations of their evidence:
- making sure that a pattern or association is checked against all the data
- showing caution in making assumptions about the general applicability of a conclusion
- finding patterns or trends in observations or results of investigations
- identifying an association between one variable and another
- making notes of observations in the course of an investigation
- using graphs, charts and tables to convey information
- choosing an appropriate means of communication that is understandable to others
- using secondary sources of information

References

▼ ▼

Centre for Studies in Science and Mathematics. (1987). *Children's Learning in Science (CLIS) Project,* Leeds University

CRIPSAT, University of Liverpool, Centre for Educational Studies, Kings College, London. (1990). *Science Processes and Concepts Exploration (SPACE)*, Liverpool University Press

Department of Education and Science. (1991). *Science in the National Curriculum (1991)*, HMSO

Harlen, W. (1992). *The Teaching of Science*, David Fulton

Harlen, W. et al, (1990). *Progress in Primary Science*, Routledge

National Curriculum Council. (1989). *Science: Non-Statutory Guidance*, NCC

Qualter, A. et al, (1990), *Exploration - A Way of Learning Science*, Blackwell

Qualter, A. (1991), 'Fair's fair', *Questions*, January 1991, pp18-19

Russell, A. (1991), 'The crucial comparisons', *Questions*, March 1991, pp20-22

Stark, R. (1991) 'The assessment of achievement programme', *Primary Science Review*, October 1991, pp18-21

The children's activities

▼ ▼

The structure of the double-page spreads

The double-page spreads which follow are each arranged in a similar pattern which reflects the process of science itself. Each spread is labelled with a science Attainment Target other than AT 1 to indicate relevant knowledge and understanding as well as a broad science theme − though this should be seen as an approximate and tentative guide for the teacher. The emphasis throughout is on activities that encourage *scientific thinking* rather than any science content. The ideas will form a flexible package that can be used alongside a variety of science schemes or cross-curricular topics.

Left-hand page: photocopiable children's material

This page provides information which can be taken as suggestions for the teacher or photocopiable material for the children. It will:

- Initiate a science investigation by providing observing activities.
- Encourage children to ask questions about the activity.
- Provide an opportunity for children to form *hypotheses* and make *predictions* based on their experiences.

During these activities children will devise and carry out informal experiments and draw conclusions as part of their observations. An activity can be:

- highly structured by asking children to follow the worksheet or
- more open-ended if the teacher discusses the ideas with children simply as a starting point.

Right-hand page: for the teacher

This page is designed for the teacher, though parts of it could be used by children as a stimulus. It contains:

- Questions that children might ask or could be encouraged to ask as a result of their initial activity.
- Possible answers that children might give to the questions in a form which can be investigated scientifically. Note that not all the suggested answers are intended to be scientifically accurate.
- Suggestions as to how one or more of the questions could be investigated, with hints on making and recording measurements.
- A list of variables that could be manipulated.
- Suggestions as to how the results might be analysed.
- Reference to the relevant parts of the Programmes of Study in Attainment Targets 2, 3, and 4.

How clean is the air?

▼ ▼

■ Can you see dust and other particles in the air?

   ● Use a torch in a darkened room or box.

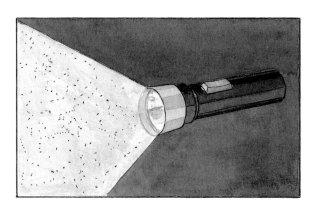

● Use a stronger light if you can.

■ Why can you see the particles more easily with a light?

■ Write down what the particles look like and what they are doing.

■ Look for dusty surfaces.

■ Make a list of where most dust is found in your classroom.

▲ TAKE CARE!
Don't touch the dust or breathe it in.
It may be harmful.

■ Write down where the dust gathers.
Explain why it gathers in these places.

■ Find out if sticky tape can be used to collect small amounts of dust from surfaces in the classroom.

How clean is the air?

▼▼▼▼▼▼▼▼▼▼▼▼▼▼▼▼▼▼▼▼▼▼▼▼▼▼▼▼▼▼▼

Attainment Target
Life and living processes
Themes
The environment,
Pollution, Air,
Weather, Change

Asking questions

Where in the air is most dust found?

What is the dust in the air made of?

Is there more dust inside a building than outside?

It might be that ...

It is near the floor in corners.
It is outside near roads.

It is made of bits of soil.

There is more inside.

Experimenting *Where in the air is most dust found?*

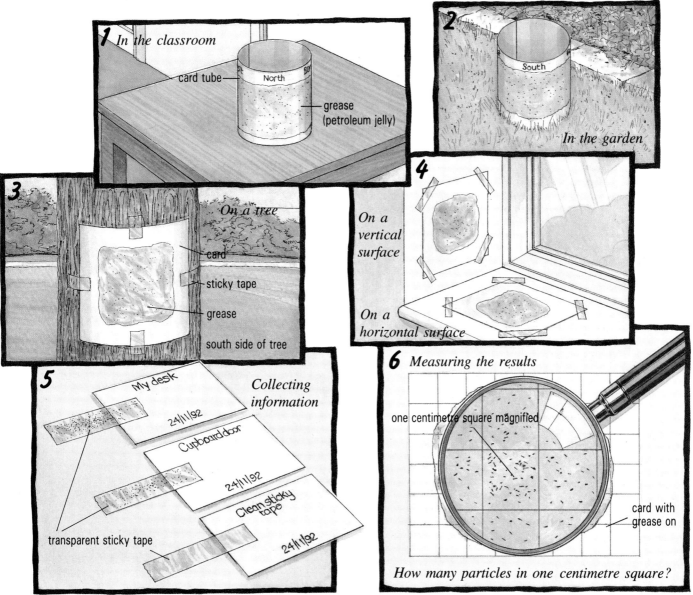

1 In the classroom — card tube — North — grease (petroleum jelly)

2 South — In the garden

3 On a tree — card — sticky tape — grease — south side of tree

4 On a vertical surface — On a horizontal surface

5 Collecting information — My desk 24/11/92 — Cupboard door 24/11/92 — Clean sticky tape 24/11/92 — transparent sticky tape

6 Measuring the results — one centimetre square magnified — card with grease on — *How many particles in one centimetre square?*

Looking at results

- *Are the same kind of particles found inside and outside the room?*
- *Are more particles found facing one particular direction, eg west?*
- *Is it possible to classify the particles: synthetic, animal?*

Variables to keep the same

- *Amount of sticky substance*
- *Area of sticky substance on card*
- *Sticky surface held horizontally or vertically?*
- *Sticky card facing same direction*

Variable to change

- *Location of sticky card*

National Curriculum

... discuss how human activity produces local changes in their environment ...study the effects of pollution on the survival of living things

How do ears hear?

▼ ▼

■ Look at a friend's ear.

■ Make a careful drawing of it, as large as you can.

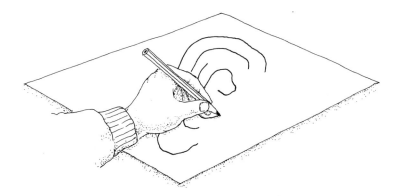

■ Ask another friend if you may draw his/her ear.

● Are the ears the same?
● How are they different?

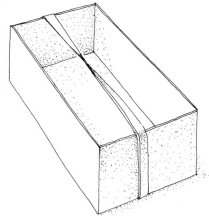

elastic band

rubber falling in jar

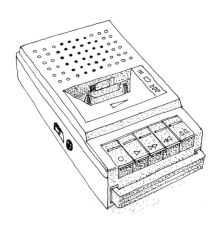

tape recorder

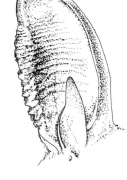

■ How well can you hear? Ask a friend to make some soft sounds to see if you can hear them.

■ How far away can you hear the sounds?

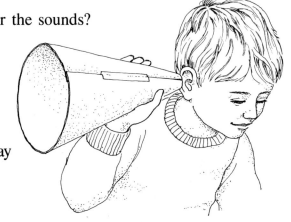

■ Make an ear trumpet to help you hear sounds.

● Can you hear the soft sounds from further away with your ear trumpet?

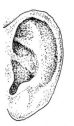

How do ears hear?

▼▼▼▼▼▼▼▼▼▼▼▼▼▼▼▼▼▼▼▼▼▼▼▼▼

Attainment Targets
Life and living
processes,
Physical processes
Themes
Ourselves, Sound,
Communications,
Toys and games,
Helping others

Asking questions

Which shape is best for an ear trumpet?

Which size is best for an ear trumpet?

It might be that ...

A bowl shape is best.

The size of the person's head is best.

Experimenting *Which shape is best for an ear trumpet?*

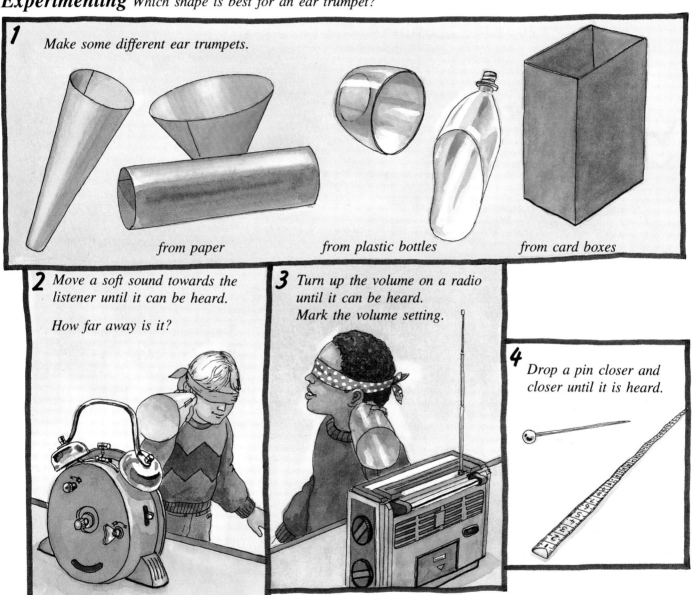

1 Make some different ear trumpets.

from paper   from plastic bottles   from card boxes

2 Move a soft sound towards the listener until it can be heard.

How far away is it?

3 Turn up the volume on a radio until it can be heard. Mark the volume setting.

4 Drop a pin closer and closer until it is heard.

Looking at results

- Is there an ear trumpet shape that seems to be best?
- How consistent and reliable is the test? If it is repeated, do you get similar results?

Variables to keep the same (frame 3)

- Material for the ear trumpet
- Radio
- Similar type of programme to listen to
- Distance from the radio
- Listener
- Ear

Variable to change

- Shape of the trumpet

National Curriculum

...develop ideas about how they grow, feed, move, use their senses ...investigate and measure the similarities and differences between themselves

Can a minibeast smell?

▼▼▼▼▼▼▼▼▼▼▼▼▼▼▼▼▼▼▼▼▼▼▼▼▼▼▼▼

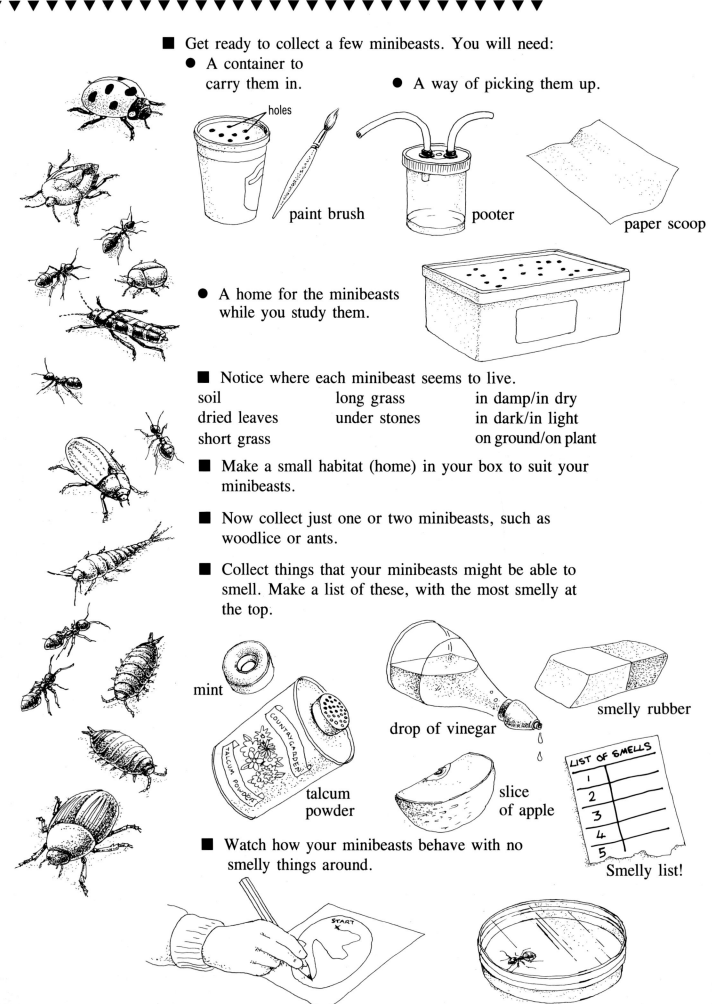

- ■ Get ready to collect a few minibeasts. You will need:
  - ● A container to carry them in.
  - ● A way of picking them up.

holes

paint brush   pooter   paper scoop

- ● A home for the minibeasts while you study them.

- ■ Notice where each minibeast seems to live.

soil	long grass	in damp/in dry
dried leaves	under stones	in dark/in light
short grass		on ground/on plant

- ■ Make a small habitat (home) in your box to suit your minibeasts.

- ■ Now collect just one or two minibeasts, such as woodlice or ants.

- ■ Collect things that your minibeasts might be able to smell. Make a list of these, with the most smelly at the top.

mint

drop of vinegar

smelly rubber

COUNTRY GARDEN
TALCUM POWDER

talcum powder   slice of apple

LIST OF SMELLS
1
2
3
4
5

Smelly list!

- ■ Watch how your minibeasts behave with no smelly things around.

START

Can a minibeast smell?

Attainment Target
Life and living processes
Themes
Minibeasts, Ourselves, The environment, Food

Asking questions

Can my minibeast smell?

Does my minibeast like some smells?

Does my minibeast hate some smells?

It might be that ...

It can smell strong smells.

It doesn't like any smells.

It does hate some synthetic smells, such as perfume.

Experimenting

1

How long will it take the minibeast to get out of the circle?
How many times should the test be tried?

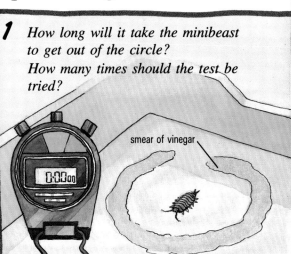

smear of vinegar

2

How does the minibeast's behaviour change in a confined space?

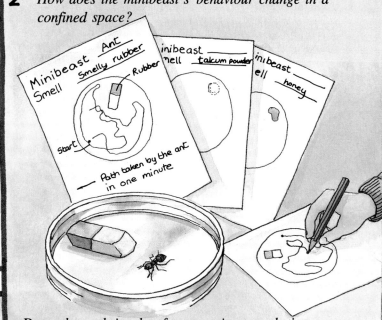

Draw the path it takes for one minute each time.

3

How far away can a smell be detected?

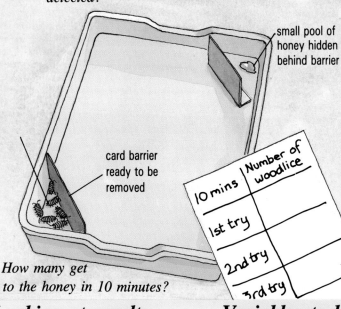

small pool of honey hidden behind barrier

card barrier ready to be removed

How many get to the honey in 10 minutes?

10 mins	Number of woodlice
1st try	
2nd try	
3rd try	

4

How many times will the minibeast escape?

card barrier removed

smear of perfume just under exit to box

Looking at results

- *Repeat the tests a number of times. How consistent are the results?*
- *Are there patterns in the way the minibeasts behave in the presence of smells?*
- *Can minibeasts smell the same things humans can?*

Variables to keep the same

- *Amount of smelly substance used*
- *Where minibeast is placed at the beginning*
- *Kind of minibeast*
- *Time of exposure to smell*

Variable to change

- *Type of smell*

National Curriculum

...study plants and animals in a variety of local habitats
...explore some aspects of
...behaviour in relation to themselves and other animals

People patterns

▼▼▼▼▼▼▼▼▼▼▼▼▼▼▼▼▼▼▼▼▼▼▼▼▼▼

■ Collect information about the children in your class.

■ Look at the information needed for this chart and
collect it for as many children as possible.

Name	Height (cm)	Distance round head (cm)	Distance round wrist (cm)	Hand span (cm)	Standing jump (cm)	Squeezing scales (kg)	Number of press-ups in 1 minute

■ How to make some of the measurements.

Hand span
The hand should be spread out as far as possible on a
flat table. Measure from the outside of the thumb to the
outside of the little finger.

Standing jump
The person stands on a line with both heels on the line.
He/she jumps as far as he/she can. Measure from the line
to where the heels land.

Squeezing scales
This is a test of the strength of the hand
and wrist. The person picks up the
bathroom scales with both hands, one
each side. He/she squeezes as hard as
possible and the best reading is taken.

■ Look for patterns in your results.

People patterns

▼ ▼

Attainment Target
Life and living
processes
Themes
Ourselves, Sport and
health, Clothes

Asking questions

Is there a connection between
people's height and how far they
can jump?

Can those with the largest hand
span squeeze the scales the best?

Do the shortest people have the
smallest heads?

Are most people around the
average height?

It might be that ...

The taller you are, the harder it is
to jump far.

The largest hands are the strongest.

There is no connection between height
and head circumference.

People's heights are spread evenly
from small to tall.

Experimenting

1 The taller you are, the harder it is
to jump far.

Use a scatter graph.

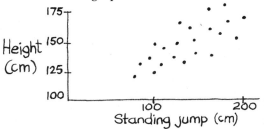

This scatter graph shows a trend:
Taller people tend to jump further.
Use a computer database or spreadsheet
to help draw scatter graphs.

2 The taller you are, the harder it is
to jump far.

Find five tall people
(from another class?)
and five short people.

Compare their
performances

3 The taller you are, the harder it is
to jump far.

How do the lists compare?

4 Are most people around the average height?

Use a histogram or frequency graph.

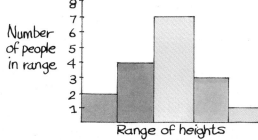

This graph shows a 'normal distribution'
of heights.

Looking at results

● Correlations: Have enough
measurements been taken to
show a viable trend? A
negative correlation will be
shown by a line sloping from
left down to right.

● Histograms: Can children
search for similar normal
distribution curves in, say,
hand spans, head circumferences
or strength tests?

Variables to keep the same (frame 2)

● Method of jumping

Variable to change

● Use different people

National Curriculum

...consider similarities and
differences between themselves
and other animals

Which colour light do plants prefer?

▼▼▼▼▼▼▼▼▼▼▼▼▼▼▼▼▼▼▼▼▼▼▼▼▼▼

■ Find different ways of getting coloured light.

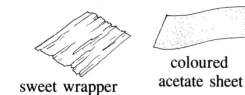

sweet wrapper
or coloured cellophane

coloured
acetate sheet

coloured glass
▲ TAKE CARE!

coloured felt pen on
clear acetate or glass

coloured liquid
(try paint or in

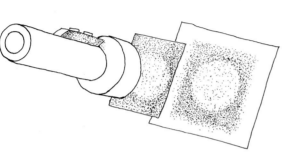

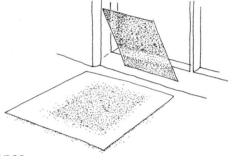

■ Try overlapping some colours to get new ones.

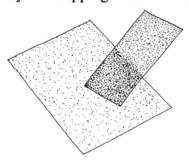

*Daylight is a mixture of **different coloured lights**. The
substances you have used allow only some of the colours
through. These substances are called **filters**.*

■ Grow some mustard or cress seedlings in daylight.

■ Use a box to make the light come from one direction.

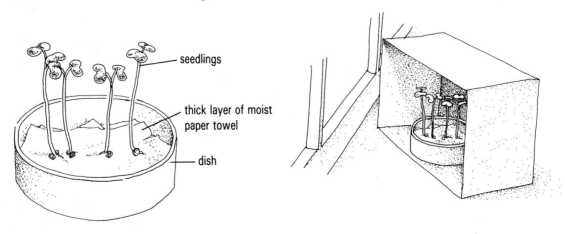

seedlings

thick layer of moist
paper towel

dish

■ Record what happens to the seedlings.

Which colour light do plants prefer?

Attainment Targets
Life and living processes, Materials and their properties, Physical processes
Themes
The environment, Growth, Colour and light, Change

▼▼▼▼▼▼▼▼▼▼▼▼▼▼▼▼▼▼▼▼▼▼▼▼▼▼▼▼▼

Asking questions

Which colour light do plants prefer?

Can plants grow in just one colour light?

Can coloured light make a plant change colour?

It might be that ...

Green light is the best.

They can grow in yellow light.

The plant becomes paler in one colour light.

Experimenting

1 *Making a coloured light environment for a plant.*

coloured sweet wrapper with tube

plastic bottle end coloured with marker

coloured paper box made translucent with oil

coloured cellophane bag

2
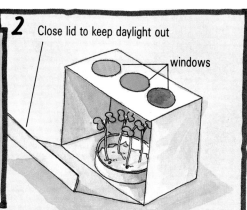
Close lid to keep daylight out
windows

3
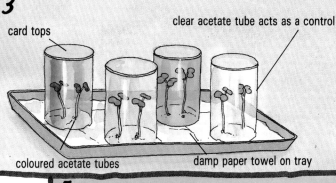
card tops
clear acetate tube acts as a control
coloured acetate tubes
damp paper towel on tray

4
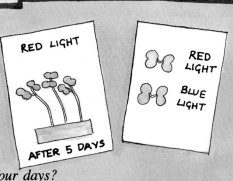

5 *Measuring and recording the results.*

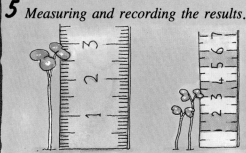
How long to grow 3 cm?   How tall in four days?

RED LIGHT
AFTER 5 DAYS

RED LIGHT
BLUE LIGHT

Looking at results

● Features of a healthy cress plant:
  dark green leaves
  upright, stout stem
  stem not elongated or stunted
● Which colour light gives these features?
● Can any of the results be repeated using a different test?

Variables to keep the same (frame 4)

● Type of seed
● Amount of water given
● Growing medium
● Intensity of light
● Temperature

Variable to change

● Colour of light

National Curriculum

... be introduced to the main parts of flowering plants and investigate what plants need to grow ...take responsibility for the care of living things ...investigate the factors that affect plant growth

Can salt stop food going bad?

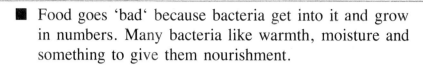

- Food goes 'bad' because bacteria get into it and grow in numbers. Many bacteria like warmth, moisture and something to give them nourishment.

- How do we stop food going bad? The table shows four ways to stop bacteria getting into food or multiplying dangerously.

- For each food, put a tick in the box which shows how it is preserved. Put more than one tick if you want.

	Keep dry	Keep cold in a fridge or freezer	Kill all bacteria then seal in a container	Keep in a liquid or other substance that bacteria don't like
Cornflakes				
Canned soup				
Packet soup				
Frozen peas				
Strawberry jam				
Pickled onions				
Bacon				
Salted fish				

- Add some more foods of your own.

Salt was used in the past to preserve some foods.

- Write down some more preservatives (substances that protect foods from bacteria).

Can salt stop food going bad?

Attainment Target
Life and living processes
Themes
Food, Shopping, Ourselves, Change, Homes, Growth

▲ *TAKE CARE! Keep deteriorating food sealed up. Dispose of it carefully.*

Asking questions

How much salt is needed to stop food going bad?

Is vinegar as good as salt at keeping food from going bad?

It might be that ...

A teaspoon in a cup of water would do.

Vinegar is more effective than salt.

Experimenting

How much salt is needed to stop food going bad?

1 Which foods to try?

slice of apple   sultanas   carrot

bread   mushroom   Oxo cube

2 Sprinkle a teaspoon of salt over food in one tray.

No Salt

Salt

damp kitchen towel

3 Try moist fruit cake. Seal the lids with sticky tape.

dry salt sprinkled on top   absorbent pad soaked in salt solution   cake under salt solution   no salt

DAY	A	B	C	D
1	Clear	Clear		
2				
3			Going Cloudy	
4				
5				

4 Place food pieces in salt solutions each made with 250 ml of water.

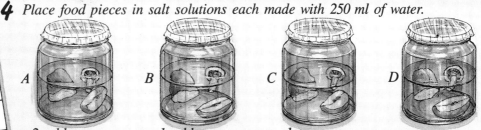

A — 2 tablespoons of salt

B — 1 tablespoon of salt

C — 1 teaspoon of salt

D — no salt

Looking at results

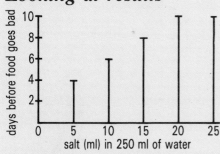

days before food goes bad (y-axis: 2, 4, 6, 8, 10)
salt (ml) in 250 ml of water (x-axis: 0, 5, 10, 15, 20, 25)

● *Do you think salt will preserve food for ever?*

● *Is there an amount of salt beyond which there is no improvement?*
● *Are all the foods in the jars affected in the same way?*

Variables to keep the same (frame 4)

● *Type of food*
● *Temperature of the food*
● *Amount of moisture present*
● *Covered or uncovered?*

Variable to change

● *Amount of salt*

National Curriculum

... study how microbes ...can affect health ...investigate the key factors in the process of decay such as temperature, moisture, air and the role of microbes

Touch testing

▼▼▼▼▼▼▼▼▼▼▼▼▼▼▼▼▼▼▼▼▼▼▼

■ Ask a partner to put some familiar things in a box.

● Can you identify each one?

■ Ask your partner to find ten secret things with surfaces that feel different.

● Don't look at them! Close your eyes or put on a blindfold.

■ Feel the surface of each object.

■ Tell your partner what you think each one is.

● Now change over and do it again.

■ Find at least six different kinds of paper.

Daily News
sugar paper
writing paper
glossy magazine
card
tissue paper

■ Spend two minutes feeling the surfaces and learning which one is which.

■ Close your eyes. Can you tell which paper is which just by feel?

Touch testing

▼▼▼▼▼▼▼▼▼▼▼▼▼▼▼▼▼▼▼▼▼▼▼▼

Attainment Targets
Life and living processes, Materials and their properties
Themes
Ourselves, Communications, Materials, Helping others

Asking questions

Who has the best sense of touch in the class?

Which is the best part of the body to touch with?

It might be that ...

It is Sally Smithers.

It is the cheek.
It is the elbow.

Experimenting Which is the most touch-sensitive part of the body?

1 Use four different grades of sandpaper.

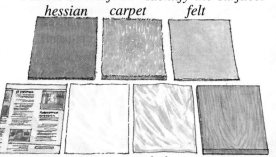

Can you put them in order?
Use: forefinger, big toe, elbow.

2 Make pin-prick patterns in paper.

Turn the paper over.
How many in each pattern?
Use: thumb, forefinger, middle finger, ring finger, little finger. Which is best?

3 Put on a blindfold. Identify the surface.

hessian   carpet   felt

newspaper   nylon   polythene   wood

4

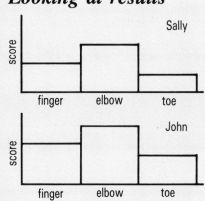

small hole
selection of test cards

How long to find the small hole in the card?

5 Don't look at the wire.
Draw its shape on paper.

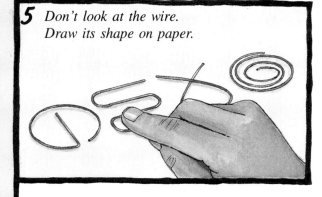

Looking at results

Sally

score — finger, elbow, toe

John

score — finger, elbow, toe

- Are there similarities in the graphs for different children?

Variables to keep the same (frame 1)

- The four grades of sandpaper
- The way the test is introduced
- Time given for the test
- Amount of previous experience with the materials

Variable to change

- The part of the body being tested

National Curriculum

...develop their ideas about how they grow, feed, move, use their senses ...investigate and measure the similarities and differences between themselves

Caring for plants

▼▼▼▼▼▼▼▼▼▼▼▼▼▼▼▼▼▼▼▼▼▼▼▼

■ Collect some different seeds and grow them on damp paper towels.

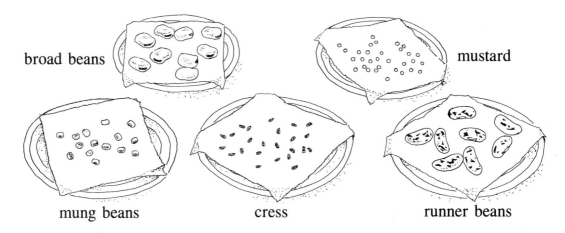

broad beans

mustard

mung beans

cress

runner beans

Use thick paper towels and keep these moist at all times.

■ Make a mini-garden with some of your seeds.

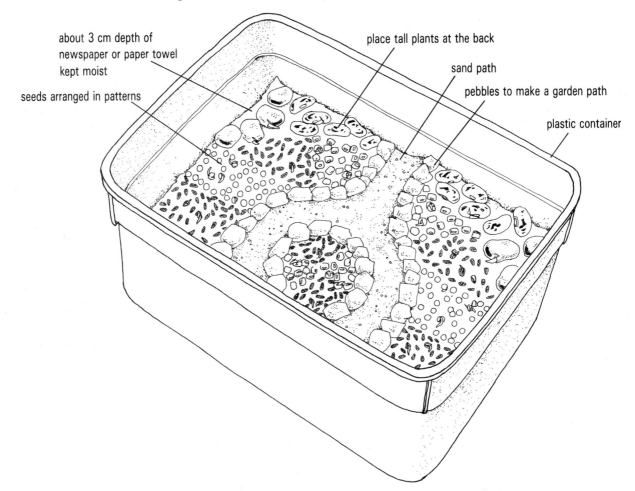

about 3 cm depth of newspaper or paper towel kept moist

seeds arranged in patterns

place tall plants at the back

sand path

pebbles to make a garden path

plastic container

■ Watch your garden grow for about three weeks.

■ What can you add to your mini-garden?

Perhaps a bench, a swing, a fence, a pond, some gnomes...

Caring for plants

▼▼▼▼▼▼▼▼▼▼▼▼▼▼▼▼▼▼▼▼▼▼▼▼▼▼▼▼▼

Attainment Target
Life and living
processes
Themes
Growth, The
environment, Change

Asking questions

*Can plants have too much or too
little of what they need?*

It might be that ...

*They can have too much water.
They can have too little water.
They can have too much warmth.
They can have too much fertiliser.*

Experimenting

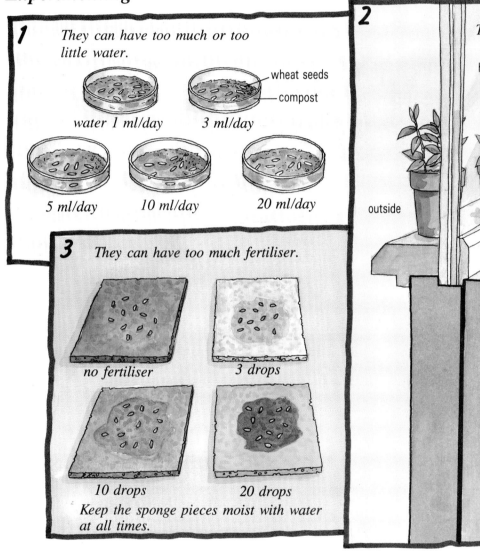

*1 They can have too much or too
little water.*

wheat seeds
compost

water 1 ml/day   3 ml/day

5 ml/day   10 ml/day   20 ml/day

3 They can have too much fertiliser.

no fertiliser   3 drops

10 drops   20 drops

*Keep the sponge pieces moist with water
at all times.*

2 They can have too much warmth.

house plant such as tradescantia

outside

Looking at results

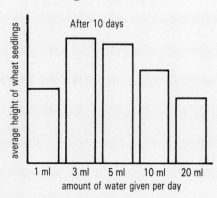

After 10 days

average height of wheat seedlings

1 ml   3 ml   5 ml   10 ml   20 ml
amount of water given per day

- *These results show wheat
seeds can be over-watered.*
- *Would similar results for
over-watering be found for
other seedlings?*

Variables to keep the same (frame 2)

- *Amount of light*
- *Type of plant*
- *Amount of water*
- *Type of compost*

Variable to change

- *Temperature around the
plants*

National Curriculum

*...investigate what plants need
to grow ...investigate the factors
that affect plant growth, for
example, light intensity,
temperature and amount of water*

Plastic bottle investigation

▼ ▼

■ You will need a clear plastic bottle with a screw cap.

■ Screw on the cap then gently squeeze the bottle. If the bottle is not airtight, find another one.

■ Blow into your bottle and feel how 'tight' it gets.

■ Suck some air out of the your bottle and feel how it draws in.

■ Pour a few centimetres of warm water into the bottle and swish it around.

■ Put the cap on quickly.

■ Draw what happens to the bottle in the next few minutes.

■ Remove the cap and listen!

■ Do the same again with cold water.

■ Do it again with cold water but this time warm the bottle under a tap or on a radiator.

■ Feel the bottle. How does it change?

■ Remove the cap and listen.

■ Put cold water in the bottle. Squeeze out a little air from the bottle before putting the cap on.

■ Watch for a few minutes then draw what happens.

Plastic bottle investigation

▼▼▼▼▼▼▼▼▼▼▼▼▼▼▼▼▼▼▼▼▼▼▼▼▼▼▼▼

Attainment Target
Materials and their
properties
Themes
Water, Air, Weather,
Hot and cold, Homes

Asking questions

Why does the wall of the bottle
move in when it contains hot
water?

Why does the wall of the bottle
move outwards when it contains
cold water?

It might be that ...

The hot water cools and contracts.
The warm air above the water
cools and contracts.
The water vapour in the bottle
condenses and contracts.

The cold water gets warmer and
expands.
The cold air above the water gets
warmer and expands.
The cold water is heavy.

Experimenting

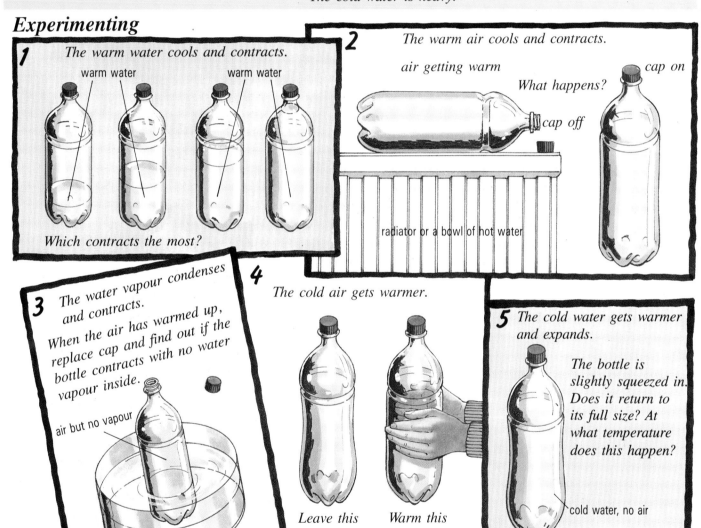

1 The warm water cools and contracts.

warm water   warm water

Which contracts the most?

2 The warm air cools and contracts.

air getting warm   What happens?   cap on

cap off

radiator or a bowl of hot water

3 The water vapour condenses and contracts.
When the air has warmed up, replace cap and find out if the bottle contracts with no water vapour inside.

air but no vapour

warm water

4 The cold air gets warmer.

Leave this bottle in the fridge.   Warm this bottle with your hands.

5 The cold water gets warmer and expands.

The bottle is slightly squeezed in. Does it return to its full size? At what temperature does this happen?

cold water, no air

Looking at results

- Do gases expand and
  contract more than liquids?

Variables to keep the same (frame 1)

- Temperature of the water
- Size of bottle
- Temperature outside the bottle

Variable to change

- The volume of water or air
  in the bottle

National Curriculum

...explore the effects of heating
some everyday substances,
compare a range of solids,
liquids and gases and recognise
the properties which enable
classification of materials in this
way

Gluing together

▼▼▼▼▼▼▼▼▼▼▼▼▼▼▼▼▼▼▼▼▼▼▼▼▼▼

■ Find some different materials.

■ Try gluing different materials together.

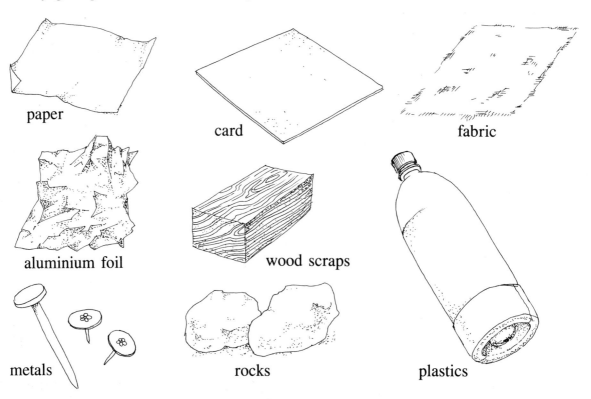

paper

card

fabric

aluminium foil

wood scraps

metals

rocks

plastics

■ Allow a day for the glue to dry, then try to pull the materials apart.

■ Record your results in a table like this. Add more rows and columns if you need them.

MATERIAL	Paper	Plastic from lemonade bottle	Iron nail	Pebble
Paper				
Plastic from lemonade bottle				
Iron nail				
Pebble				

■ In each box write one of the following:
S for strong
M for medium strength or
W for weak

■ Which materials are joined strongly by the glue?

Gluing together

▼▼▼▼▼▼▼▼▼▼▼▼▼▼▼▼▼▼▼▼▼▼▼▼▼▼

Asking questions

Which glue is the strongest?

Is glue just as strong when it is diluted?

It might be that ...

Wallpaper paste is best.

It is just as strong when a small amount of water is added.

Experimenting *Which glue is the strongest?*

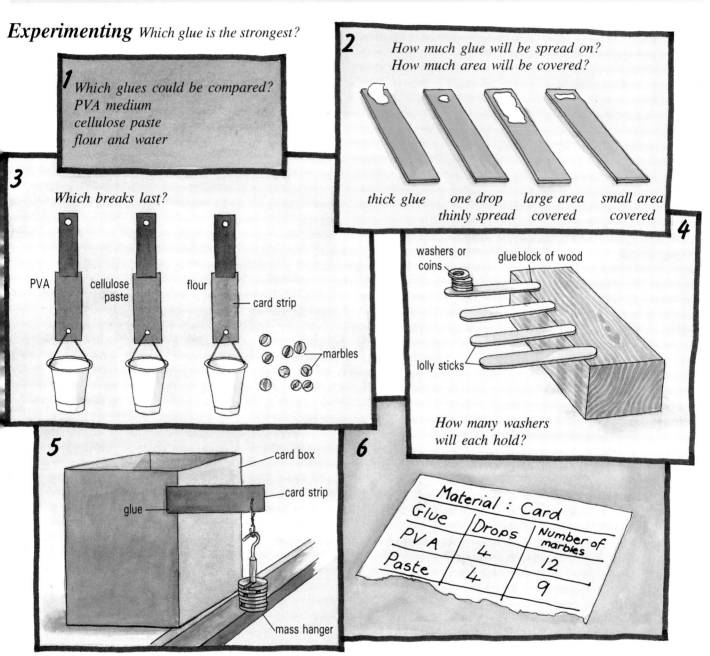

1 Which glues could be compared?
PVA medium
cellulose paste
flour and water

2 How much glue will be spread on?
How much area will be covered?

thick glue — one drop thinly spread — large area covered — small area covered

3 Which breaks last?

PVA — cellulose paste — flour — card strip — marbles

4 washers or coins — glue block of wood — lolly sticks
How many washers will each hold?

5 card box — card strip — glue — mass hanger

6

Material : Card		
Glue	Drops	Number of marbles
PVA	4	12
Paste	4	9

Looking at results

● *Did all the glues give way? If not, use a smaller area or less glue to get a result.*

● *How much stronger is PVA than flour and water?*

Variables to keep the same (frame 4)

● *Material being glued*
● *Amount of glue used*
● *Area covered by glue*
● *Way in which material is pulled apart*

Variable to change

● *Type of glue*

National Curriculum

*...investigate a number of different everyday materials
...Properties such as strength
...should be investigated and related to everyday uses of the materials*

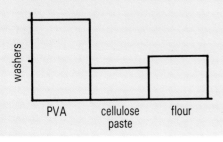

washers

PVA — cellulose paste — flour

Ice cubes

▼ ▼ ▼ ▼ ▼ ▼ ▼ ▼ ▼ ▼ ▼ ▼ ▼ ▼ ▼ ▼ ▼ ▼ ▼ ▼

Read all of this sheet before you get your ice cube.

■ Look at an ice cube on a dish. What can you see
  ● on the surface of the ice?
  ● inside the ice?

■ Close your eyes. What does the ice feel like
  ● when you touch it gently?
  ● when you press harder with your fingers?

■ Take a paper clip and straighten it out.

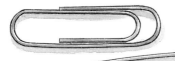

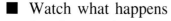

■ Hold the paper clip steadily across the ice cube and
  press down a little.

■ Watch what happens
  ● after a minute
  ● after three minutes.

■ Can you pick the paper clip up now?

■ Draw a picture of what has happened.

■ Write down what has happened and try to explain
  why.

■ Hold some thread or plastic coated electrical wire
  across the ice cube in the same way.
  ● Describe how this is different.

*Materials that melt the ice easily carry the heat from the
room or your finger to the ice. These materials are called
conductors.*
*Materials that don't carry the heat so easily are called
insulators.*

Ice cubes

▼▼▼▼▼▼▼▼▼▼▼▼▼▼▼▼▼▼▼▼▼▼▼▼▼▼

Asking questions

How can we slow down the melting of ice in the classroom?

It might be that ...

It can be wrapped in newspaper.
It can be surrounded by water.
It can be covered in sheep's wool.
It can be put in a lot of polythene bags.

Attainment Targets
Materials and their properties, Physical processes
Themes
The seasons, Hot and cold, Water, Weather, The pond, Homes, Food, Change

Experimenting

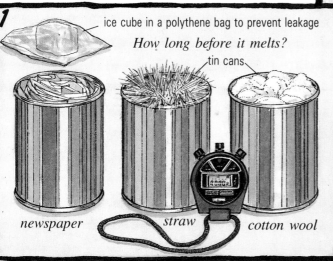

1 ice cube in a polythene bag to prevent leakage

How long before it melts?

tin cans

newspaper   straw   cotton wool

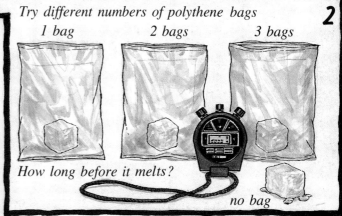

2 Try different numbers of polythene bags

1 bag   2 bags   3 bags

How long before it melts?   no bag

3

Which melts first?

polystyrene
ice cube
dish
cork

4 Can a liquid insulate an ice cube?
How big are the cubes after ½ hour?

tap water at room temperature   cooking oil at room temperature

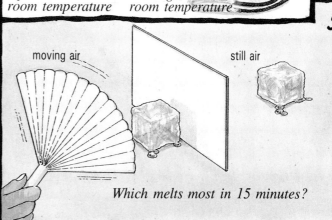

5

moving air   still air

Which melts most in 15 minutes?

Looking at results

- *What are the features of the best insulator?*
- *Does moving air make a difference to the rate of melting?*

Variables to keep the same (frame 2)

- *Size of cube*
- *Starting time*
- *Size of bags*
- *Temperature of location in room*

Variable to change

- *Number of polythene bags*

National Curriculum

...explore the effects of heating some everyday substances, for example, ice ...compare a range of solids, liquids

Ink gardens

▼▼▼▼▼▼▼▼▼▼▼▼▼▼▼▼▼▼▼▼▼▼▼▼▼

You will need some strips of absorbent material, such as blotting paper, paper towel or (coffee) filter paper.

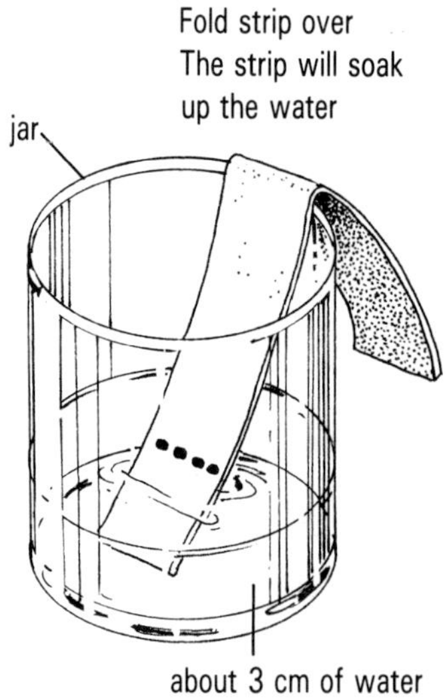

Fold strip over
The strip will soak up the water

jar

about 3 cm of water

■ Make a 'garden' of coloured felt pen dots.

strip of absorbent material about 3 cm wide

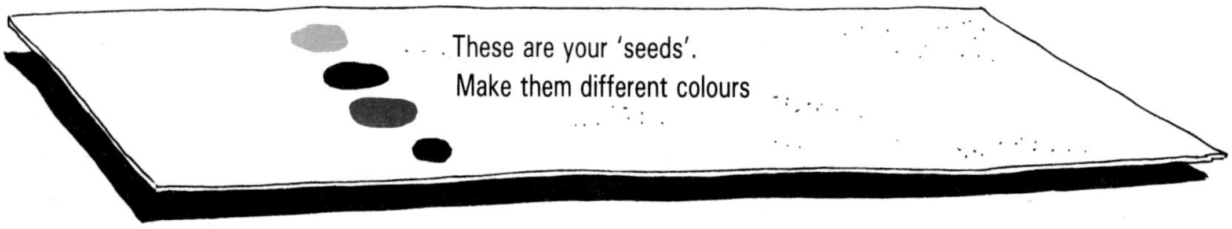

These are your 'seeds'.
Make them different colours

■ Put your strip in a container of water and watch your garden grow.

■ Try these 'gardens'.

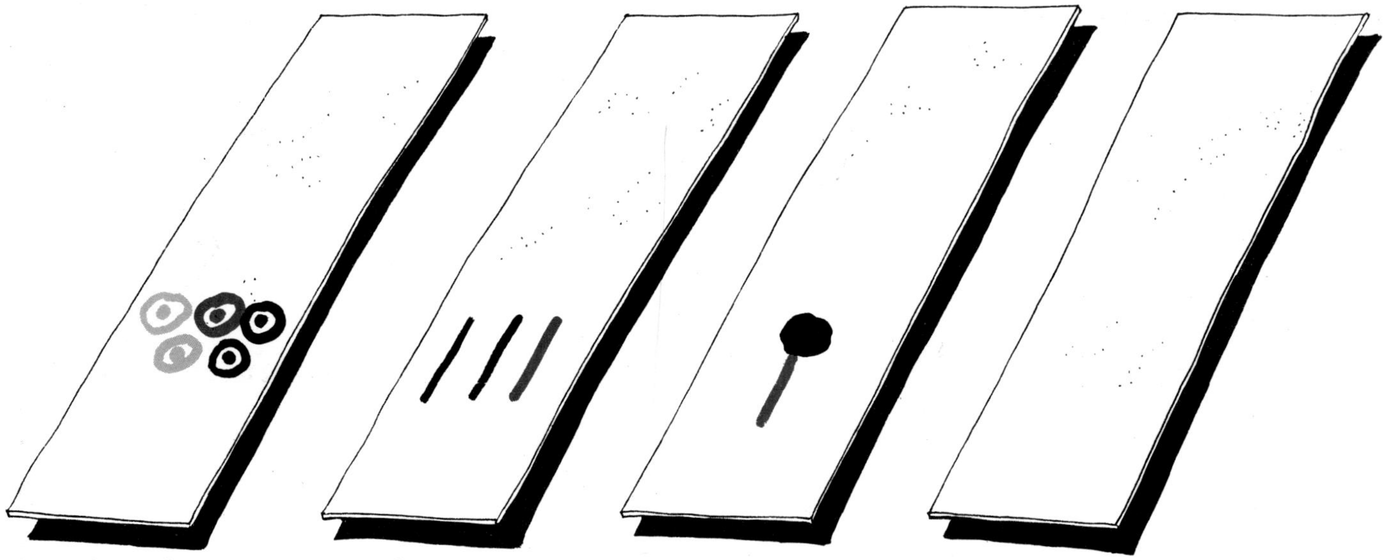

coloured
dots in circles

coloured
'plant sticks'

coloured flower,
green stem

Try some ideas
of your own.

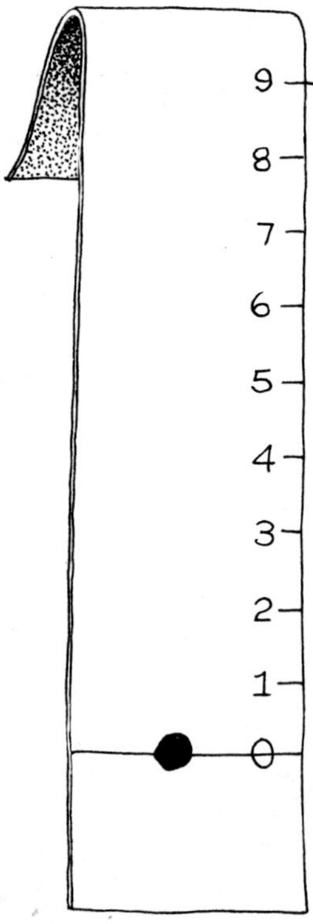

Mark centimetre spaces in pencil

9
8
7
6
5
4
3
2
1
0

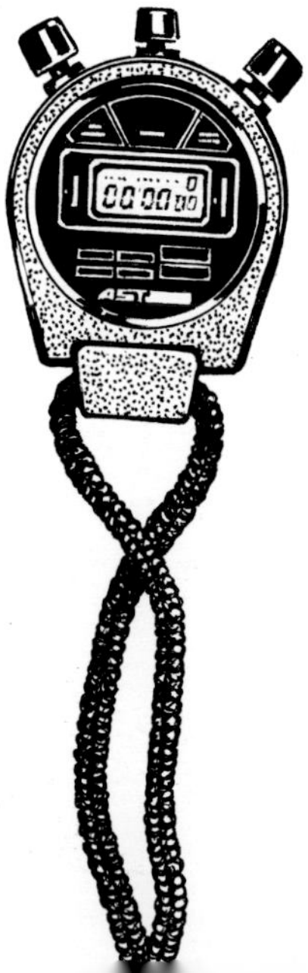

■ How fast does an 'ink plant' grow?

■ Fill in this table as your ink plant grows.

Height of ink mark (cm)	Time to get there (seconds)		
	1st try	2nd try	3rd try
2			
4			
6			
8			

● If your ink plant could grow to 10 cm, how long do you think it would take?

58

Ink gardens

Asking questions	It might be that ...
Can the 'ink plant' grow over the side of the container?	The ink will not go over the edge.
Can the ink grow horizontally?	It cannot grow horizontally.
Is it possible to stop the ink with a wax crayon line?	It is possible to stop the ink flow.
Can I slow the ink down in some way?	It is possible by using a lot of strips at the same time.
How can I make the 'plant' grow in the other direction?	It is possible by holding it out of the water for a while.
Can I get new colours by mixing the dots?	It is possible to get green from blue and yellow dots merging.

Experimenting

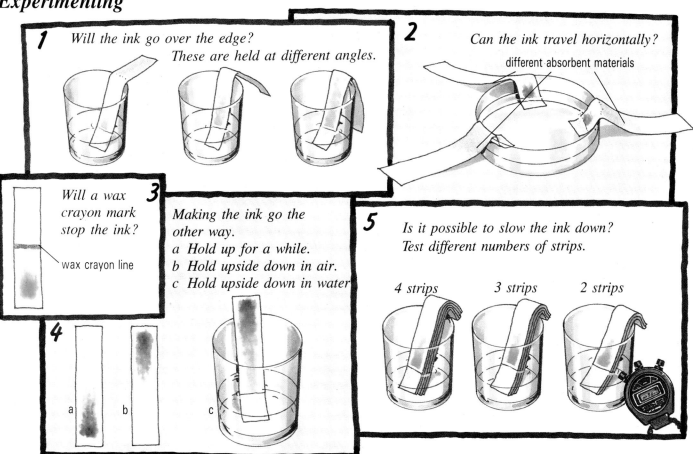

1 Will the ink go over the edge?
These are held at different angles.

2 Can the ink travel horizontally?
different absorbent materials

3 Will a wax crayon mark stop the ink?
wax crayon line

Making the ink go the other way.
a Hold up for a while.
b Hold upside down in air.
c Hold upside down in water

4 a b c

5 Is it possible to slow the ink down?
Test different numbers of strips.

4 strips   3 strips   2 strips

Looking at results

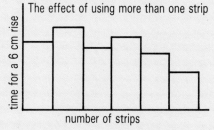

The effect of using more than one strip

time for a 6 cm rise

number of strips

- Are the results consistent?
- Compare the general shapes of the graphs for other materials.

Variables to keep the same (frame 5)

- Size of each strip
- Type and size of ink dot
- Depth of water in container
- Distance over which dot is timed
- Material used

Variable to change

- Number of strips

National Curriculum

...explore the properties of ...materials referring, for example, to their colour and texture ...explore ways of separating mixtures by using ...chromatography

Jelly watching

▼▼▼▼▼▼▼▼▼▼▼▼▼▼▼▼▼▼▼▼▼▼▼▼▼▼

■ Try this.

▲ TAKE CARE!

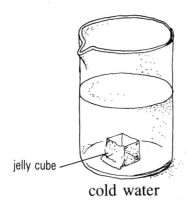
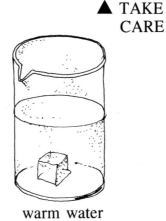

jelly cube — cold water   warm water   hot water

■ Gently put the jelly cubes in the water. Try not to move the water too much.

■ Watch the cubes for about 10 minutes.

■ Draw what happens.

■ Stir the cubes for 100 stirs.

■ Draw what has happened now.

■ Try to explain, in writing, why this happened.

*Some of the jelly has **dissolved** in the water.*

Sugar watching

cold water   warm water

■ Get two clean drinking glasses and a tablespoon. Wash your hands.

■ Gently pour sugar in the water. Try not to move the water too much.

■ Watch the sugar grains carefully. Use a hand lens if you can.

■ Record what happens in each glass. Record the differences between the two.

■ Ask your teacher if you can taste the water in each glass after 15 minutes.

■ Write down what you notice.

*Some of the sugar has **dissolved** in the water.*

Jelly watching

▼ ▼

Attainment Target
Materials and their
properties
Themes
The kitchen, Homes,
Water, Food, Change

Asking questions

What makes things dissolve faster?

*What happens when the jelly is cut
into smaller pieces?*

It might be that ...

*It is a greater volume of water that
makes things dissolve faster.
It is a higher water temperature.
It is the number of stirs given.*

It dissolves faster.

Experimenting What makes things dissolve faster?

1 *It is a greater volume of water that
makes things dissolve faster.*

*How long does each take to
dissolve completely?*

sugar in warm water   salt in warm water   jelly in warm water

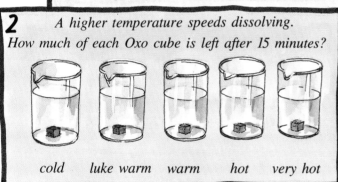

2 *A higher temperature speeds dissolving.
How much of each Oxo cube is left after 15 minutes?*

cold   luke warm   warm   hot   very hot

3 *Investigate temperature and stirring.
How long before the salt disappears?*

tablespoon of salt

cold tap water   hot tap water

4 *Investigate temperature and shaking.*

*How many shakes before the salt
disappears?*

*Repeat for water at 25°, 20°
and 15°C.*

water
at 30° C

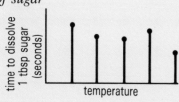

Looking at results

*How temperature affects the time
it takes to dissolve one tablespoon
of sugar*

time to dissolve
1 tbsp sugar
(seconds)

temperature

- *If the number of stirs is
  doubled, is the dissolving
  time halved?*

- *If the temperature is doubled,
  is the dissolving time halved?*
- *Does the amount that has to
  be dissolved slow down the
  rate of dissolving?*

Variables to keep the same (frame 1)

- *Amount of substance to be
  dissolved*
- *Size of container*

- *Temperature of the water*
- *Stillness of the water*

Variable to change

- *Volume of water*

National Curriculum

*...see how some (substances)
can be changed by simple
processes such as dissolving
...Properties such as ...solubility
should be investigated*

Going rusty

■ Collect some things that have gone rusty.

■ Draw some of your collection.

■ Look around your school for rusty things. Make a record chart like this one.

RUST SURVEY			
Rusty thing	What is it made of ?	Where was it found ?	How much is covered in rust all/most/a bit?
Old garden tool			

● What are all the rusty things made from?

● Where are most rusty things found?

● Can some rust be scraped off or washed off?

■ Look at some rust with a hand lens or microscope.

■ Draw some rust. Try to get the colours right.

*Things made from **iron** go rusty.*

Going rusty

▼▼▼▼▼▼▼▼▼▼▼▼▼▼▼▼▼▼▼▼▼▼▼▼▼▼▼▼

Attainment Target
Materials and their
properties
Themes
Weather, Water,
Metals, Buildings,
Homes, Change

Asking questions

What makes things go rusty?

What stops things going rusty?

It might be that ...

It is water.
It is the gases in the air.
It is acid rain.
It is air and water together.

It is paint.
It is grease.
It is when they are kept dry.

Experimenting *What makes things go rusty?*

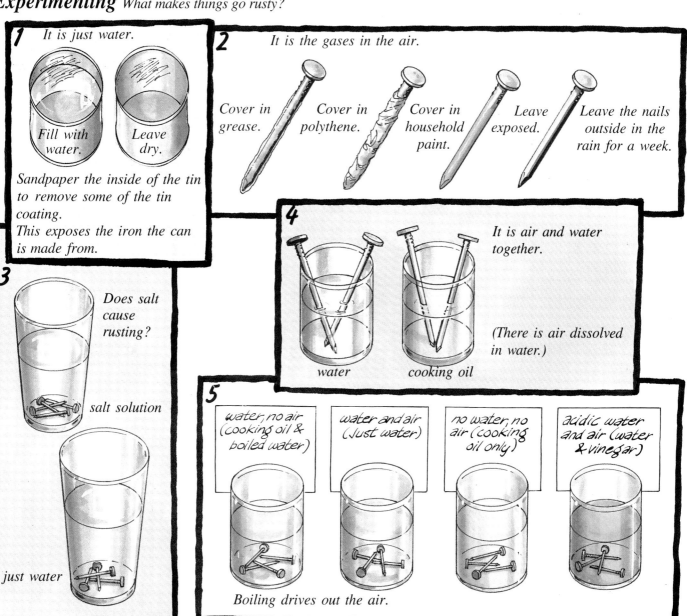

1 *It is just water.*

Fill with water. | Leave dry.

Sandpaper the inside of the tin to remove some of the tin coating.
This exposes the iron the can is made from.

2 *It is the gases in the air.*

Cover in grease. | Cover in polythene. | Cover in household paint. | Leave exposed. | Leave the nails outside in the rain for a week.

3 Does salt cause rusting?

salt solution

just water

4 *It is air and water together.*

(There is air dissolved in water.)

water | cooking oil

5

water, no air (cooking oil & boiled water) | water and air (just water) | no water, no air (cooking oil only) | acidic water and air (water & vinegar)

Boiling drives out the air.

Looking at results

- Which ingredients are required to form rust?
- Which ingredients accelerate the formation of rust?
- Do these agree with the observations made around the home and school?

Variables to keep the same (frame 1)

- Thing that might go rusty
- Time of exposure
- Exposure conditions

Variable to change

- Amount of water present

National Curriculum

...explore chemical changes in a number of everyday materials such as ...when iron rusts

63

Pouring spouts

▼▼▼▼▼▼▼▼▼▼▼▼▼▼▼▼▼▼▼▼▼▼

■ Look at different spouts. How do they pour?

   ● Do some of them drip?

■ How slowly can you pour without dribbling?

■ Draw a large picture of four different spouts.

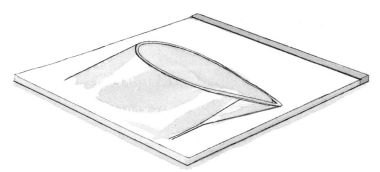

■ How slowly can you fill a cup from a container with a spout?

   ● Use a timer to find out.

   ● You must keep the water flowing!

Pouring spouts

▼▼▼▼▼▼▼▼▼▼▼▼▼▼▼▼▼▼▼▼▼▼▼▼▼▼

Attainment Target
Materials and their
properties
Themes
Water, Homes

Asking questions

Which shaped spout is best for
pouring slowly?

Why do some spouts dribble?

It might be that ...

One with a long lip is best.

They have too thick an edge to the
lip.

Experimenting Which shaped spout is best for pouring slowly?

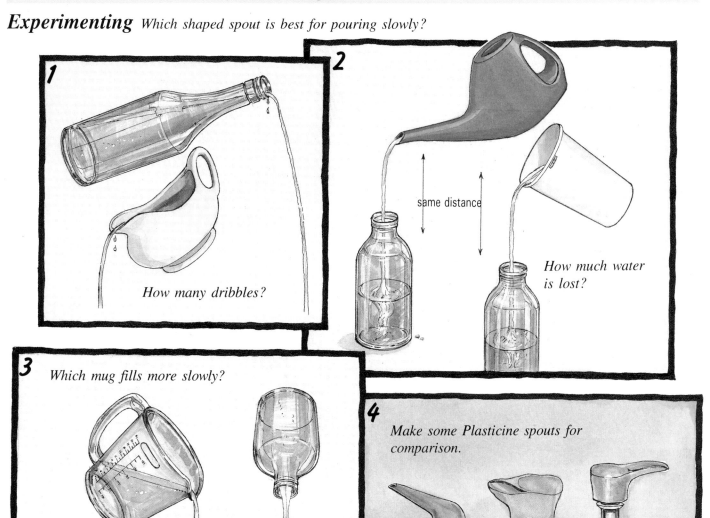

1 How many dribbles?

2 same distance — How much water is lost?

3 Which mug fills more slowly?

4 Make some Plasticine spouts for comparison.

Looking at results

- What are the characteristics
  of the most successful spouts?
- Does the thickness of the
  spout edge make a difference?
- Does the shape of the spout
  edge make a difference?
- Does the size of the container
  make a difference?

Variables to keep the same

- Person doing the pouring
- Volume of water in pouring
  container
- Distance poured
- Container to be filled

Variable to change

- Type of spout

National Curriculum

...explore the properties of
...materials ...consider some of
their everyday uses ...see how
some can be changed by simple
processes such as pouring

Can you see through paper?

■ Collect eight different kinds of paper.

tissue

newspaper

paper towel

magazine

■ Which ones can you see some light through?

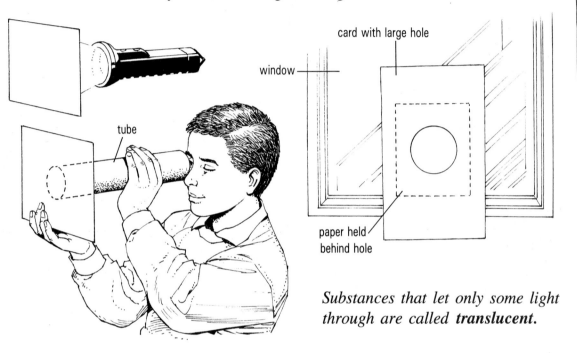

card with large hole

window

tube

paper held behind hole

Substances that let only some light through are called **translucent.**

■ Do some of your papers let more light through than others?

■ Try to arrange your eight kinds of paper in order of their translucency.

■ Cut eight holes in a strip of card.

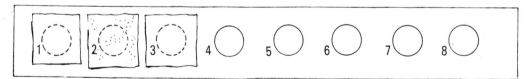

■ Glue a small piece of each paper over each hole in the card in the order you have put them.
  ● Hold your card up to the light. Does it go from lighter to darker?

Can you see through paper?

Attainment Targets
Materials and their properties, Physical processes
Themes
Light and colour, Materials, Paper, Ourselves

Asking questions

Which substances could we put on paper to make it more translucent?

Is it possible to see some writing through paper that has been made translucent?

It might be that ...

Water or grease might be best.

It is possible if the writing is held up close.

Experimenting   Which substances could we put on paper to make it more translucent?

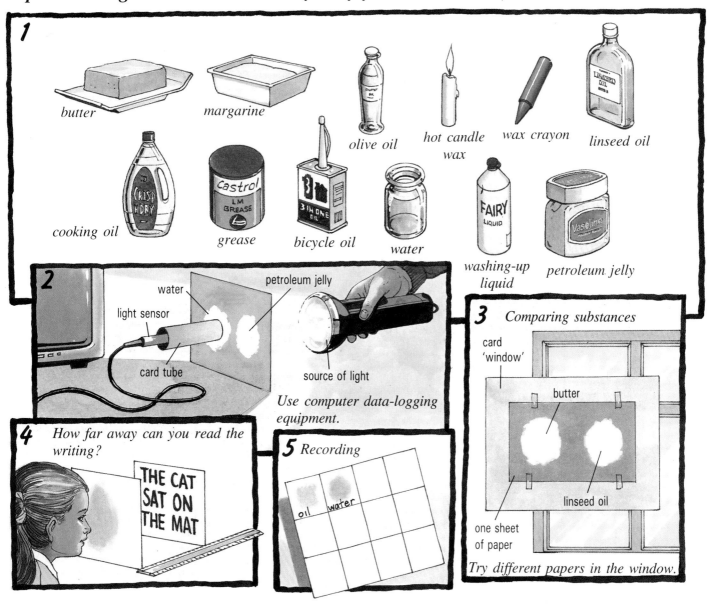

1
butter   margarine   olive oil   hot candle wax   wax crayon   linseed oil

cooking oil   grease   bicycle oil   water   washing-up liquid   petroleum jelly

2
light sensor   water   petroleum jelly   source of light
card tube
Use computer data-logging equipment.

3 Comparing substances
card 'window'   butter
linseed oil
one sheet of paper
Try different papers in the window.

4 How far away can you read the writing?
THE CAT SAT ON THE MAT

5 Recording
oil   water

Looking at results

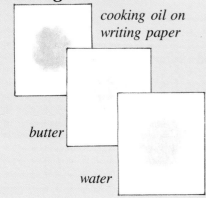

cooking oil on writing paper

butter

water

- Can the substances be placed in order?
- What do the 'best' substances have in common?

Variables to keep the same

- Amount of substance on the paper
- Type of paper
- Light behind paper
- Method of measuring light

Variable to change

- Type of substance

National Curriculum

...explore the properties of ...materials ...opportunities to explore light ...explore the effects produced by shining light through ...objects.

Waterproofing

▼▼▼▼▼▼▼▼▼▼▼▼▼▼▼▼▼▼▼▼▼▼▼▼▼▼▼

■ Make a collection of different fabrics.

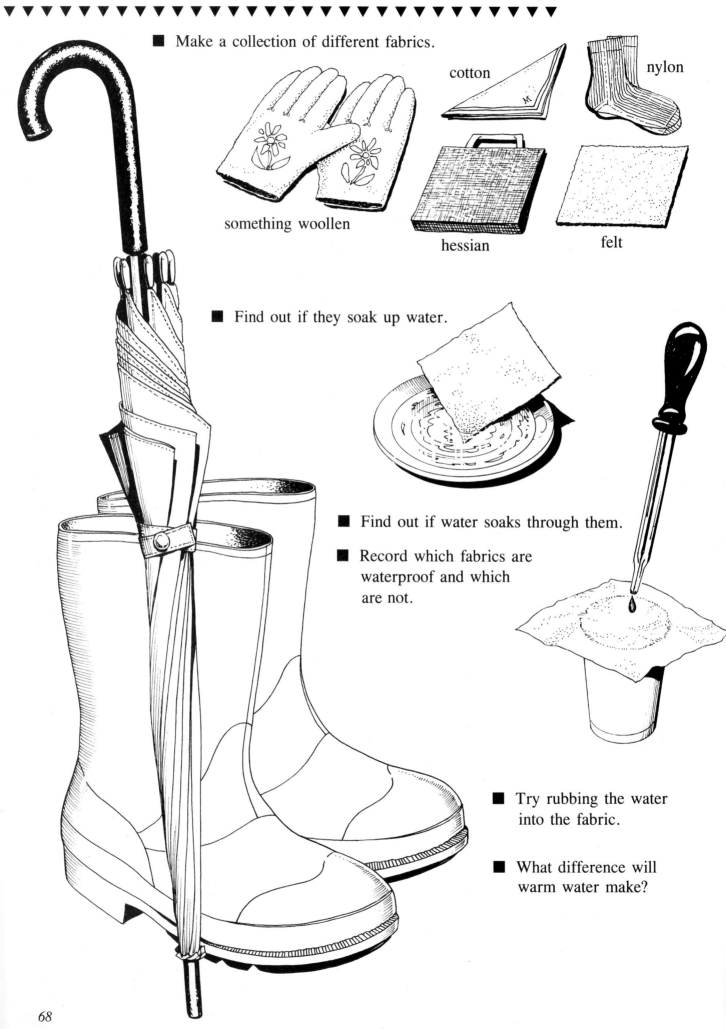

cotton

nylon

something woollen

hessian

felt

■ Find out if they soak up water.

■ Find out if water soaks through them.

■ Record which fabrics are
waterproof and which
are not.

■ Try rubbing the water
into the fabric.

■ What difference will
warm water make?

Waterproofing

▼▼▼▼▼▼▼▼▼▼▼▼▼▼▼▼▼▼▼▼▼▼▼▼▼

Attainment Target
Materials and their
properties
Themes
Seasons, Weather,
Clothes, Water

Asking questions

Is it possible to make paper
water proof?

What difference does detergent
make to waterproofing?

It might be that ...

It is, with wax crayon rubbed on
the surface.

It destroys the waterproofing
effect.

Experimenting

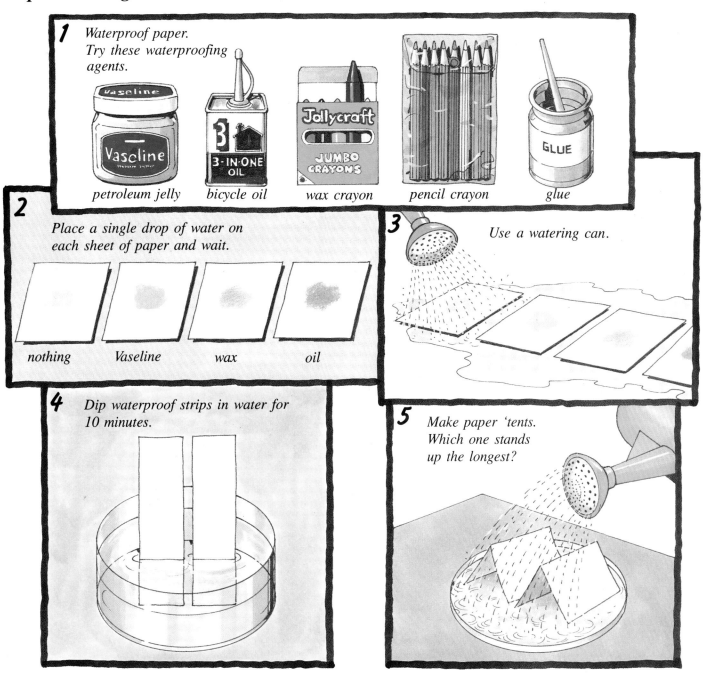

1 Waterproof paper.
Try these waterproofing
agents.

petroleum jelly   bicycle oil   wax crayon   pencil crayon   glue

2 Place a single drop of water on
each sheet of paper and wait.

nothing   Vaseline   wax   oil

3 Use a watering can.

4 Dip waterproof strips in water for
10 minutes.

5 Make paper 'tents.
Which one stands
up the longest?

Looking at results

- What do the waterproofing
  agents have in common?

Variables to keep the same (frame 5)

- Size and shape of each tent
- Amount of water poured on
  each tent
- Force of water on each tent

Variable to change

- Waterproofing on each tent

National Curriculum

...explore the properties of
materials ...and consider some
of their everyday uses

69

Which toy parachute?

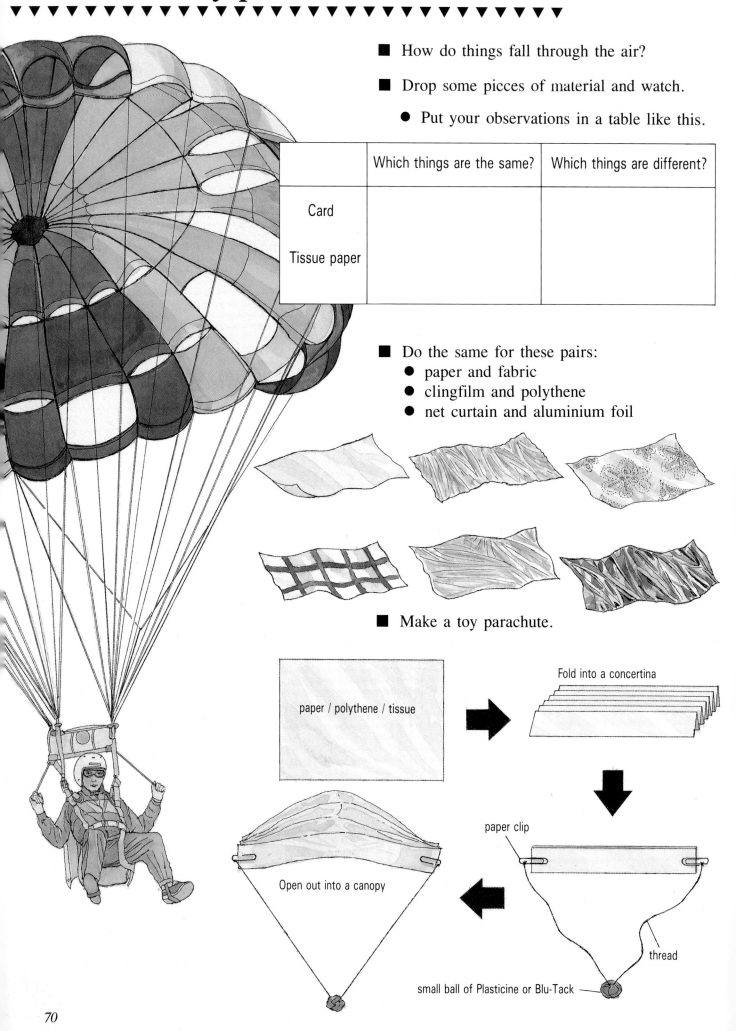

- How do things fall through the air?

- Drop some pieces of material and watch.
  - Put your observations in a table like this.

	Which things are the same?	Which things are different?
Card		
Tissue paper		

- Do the same for these pairs:
  - paper and fabric
  - clingfilm and polythene
  - net curtain and aluminium foil

- Make a toy parachute.

paper / polythene / tissue

Fold into a concertina

paper clip

thread

small ball of Plasticine or Blu-Tack

Open out into a canopy

Which toy parachute?

Attainment Targets
Materials and their properties, Physical processes
Themes
Flight, Air, Moving things, Toys and games, Transport, Space exploration

Asking questions

Which is the best material for the parachute?

Which is the best shape for the parachute?

Which is the best size rectangle for the parachute?

Would a hole in the top make a difference to its flight?

It might be that ...

Aluminium foil is the best material.

A square is the best shape.

The size of a newspaper page is best.

It makes no difference to the flight.

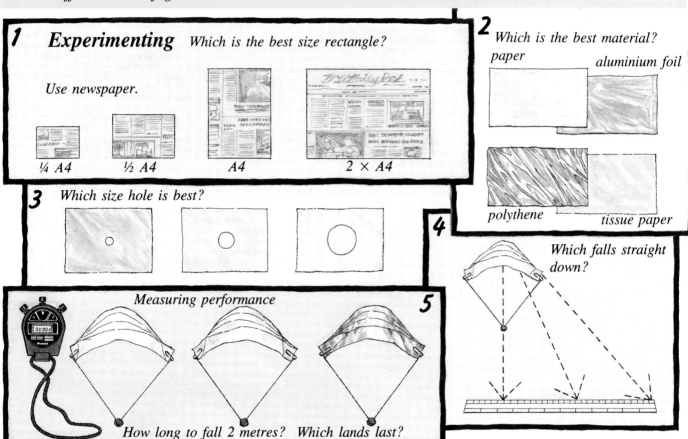

1 Experimenting Which is the best size rectangle?

Use newspaper.

¼ A4   ½ A4   A4   2 × A4

2 Which is the best material?

paper   aluminium foil

polythene   tissue paper

3 Which size hole is best?

4

Which falls straight down?

5 Measuring performance

How long to fall 2 metres?   Which lands last?

Looking at results

- Record order of landing.

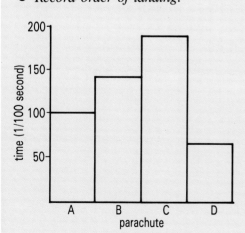

time (1/100 second)

200
150
100
50

A   B   C   D
parachute

best size for canopy

time

size of canopy

- Is there an optimum size for the hole or canopy?
- Is it possible to predict the optimum size without making the parachute? (Use a scattergraph.)
- Can a computer database help if you have a lot of results?

- Use a computer database.

Variables to keep the same (frame 3)

- Parachute material
- Size of material
- Length of thread
- Size of weight
- Method and height of launch
- Shape of hole

Variable to change

- Size of hole

National Curriculum

...experience the natural force of gravity pulling things down
...investigate movement using a variety of devices, for example toys and models

Drying out

▼▼▼▼▼▼▼▼▼▼▼▼▼▼▼▼▼▼▼▼▼▼▼▼▼▼▼

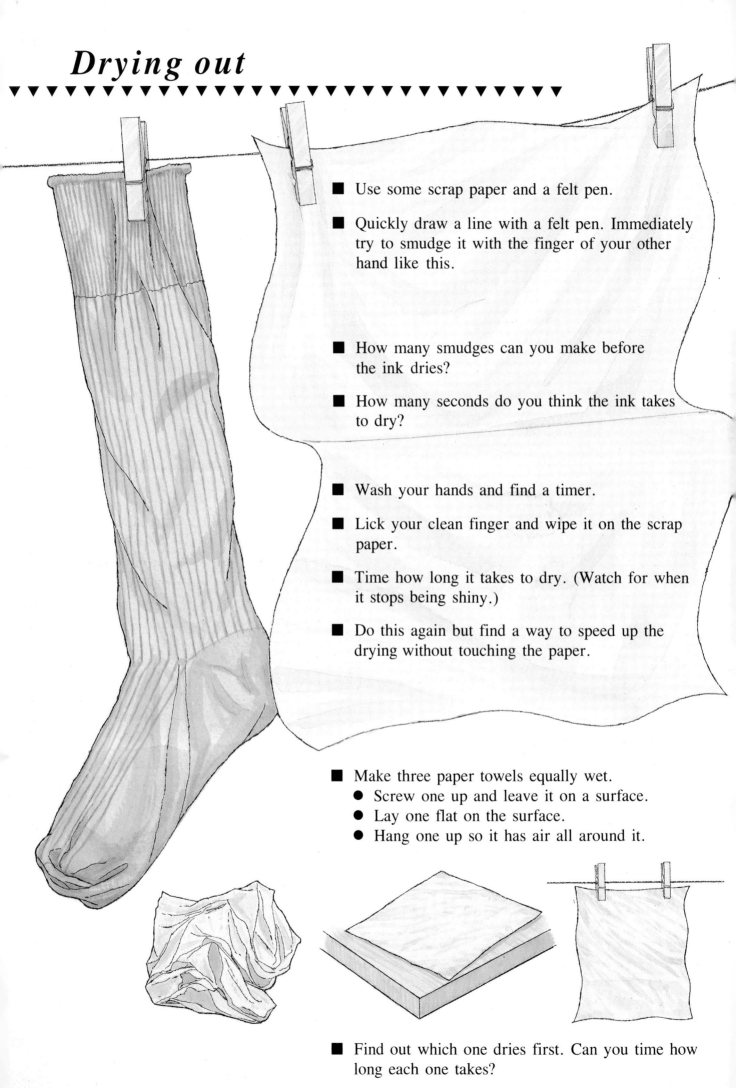

■ Use some scrap paper and a felt pen.

■ Quickly draw a line with a felt pen. Immediately try to smudge it with the finger of your other hand like this.

■ How many smudges can you make before the ink dries?

■ How many seconds do you think the ink takes to dry?

■ Wash your hands and find a timer.

■ Lick your clean finger and wipe it on the scrap paper.

■ Time how long it takes to dry. (Watch for when it stops being shiny.)

■ Do this again but find a way to speed up the drying without touching the paper.

■ Make three paper towels equally wet.
  ● Screw one up and leave it on a surface.
  ● Lay one flat on the surface.
  ● Hang one up so it has air all around it.

■ Find out which one dries first. Can you time how long each one takes?

Drying out

Asking questions

What helps water to evaporate?

It might be that ...

It is a high temperature.
It is still air.
It is the shape of the container.
It is the area of the water surface.
It is being outside the classroom.

What slows down evaporation?   It is a low temperature.

Where does the water in a puddle go?   It disappears into air.

Experimenting *What helps water to evaporate?*

1 *It is a high temperature.*

Put in the fridge.   Put on a radiator.

Put outside in a shelter.   Keep in the classroom.

Look at and mark the levels each day.

2 *It is still air.*   paper towel   This one is kept in still air.

wet spot   Use as a fan.

Which dries first? Or which dries most in 10 minutes?

It is the shape of the container.

How much evaporates in a week?

Keep exposed area the same.

4 *It is the area of the exposed water surface.*

Which dries out first?

Use the same volume of water in each.

Looking at results

- Is there a connection between the average temperature and the amount of water lost?
- Use a scatter graph.

[scatter graph: y-axis "depth lost in one day (cm)", x-axis "average temperature of water (°C)"]

Variables to keep the same (frame 4)

- Temperature around each container
- Movement of air around each container
- Volume of water at the beginning

Variable to change

- Surface area of water

National Curriculum

Experiments on ...evaporation should lead to developing ideas about solutions and solubility ...explore ways of separating and purifying mixtures ...by using evaporation

Floating and sinking

■ Find some things that float.

blocks of wood   *table tennis ball*   *polystyrene tray*   *cotton reel*   *wooden rod with Plasticine at one end*

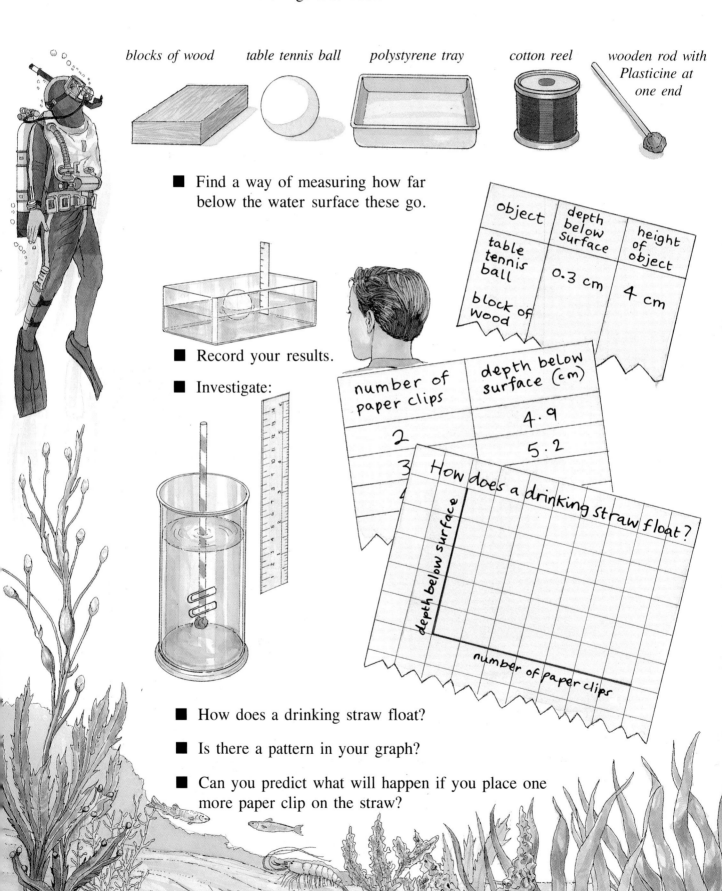

■ Find a way of measuring how far below the water surface these go.

object	depth below surface	height of object
table tennis ball	0.3 cm	4 cm
block of wood		

■ Record your results.

■ Investigate:

number of paper clips	depth below surface (cm)
	4.9
2	5.2
3	

How does a drinking straw float?

depth below surface

number of paper clips

■ How does a drinking straw float?

■ Is there a pattern in your graph?

■ Can you predict what will happen if you place one more paper clip on the straw?

Floating and sinking

▼ ▼

Attainment Target
Physical processes
Themes
Water, Transport,
Journeys, Forces

Asking questions	*It might be that ...*
Why do things sink?	*They are too heavy.*
	They are made from metal.
	They are too big.
	It is because of their shape.
Why do things float?	*They are light.*
	They are made from wood.
	They contain air.
	They have a certain shape.
Does water push upwards on things that sink?	*It only pushes upwards on things that float.*

Experimenting Why do things sink?

1 *They are too heavy.*
Find as many tiny things as you can that sink.

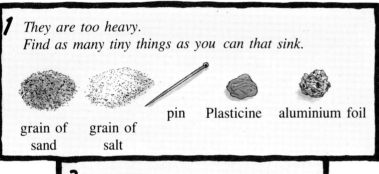

grain of sand   grain of salt   pin   Plasticine   aluminium foil

2 *They are made from metal.*
Make a list of non-metallic sinkers.

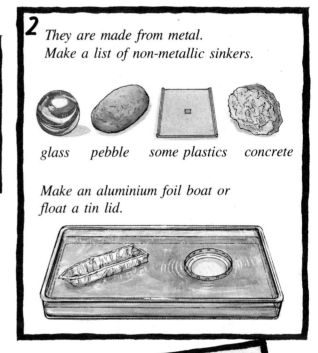

glass   pebble   some plastics   concrete

Make an aluminium foil boat or float a tin lid.

3

They are too big.
Watch small grains of soil settle in water. How long does the last one take?

Experimenting Why do things float?

4
They are light.
Make a list of very light things that sink.

5 *They have a certain shape.*
Find as many differently shaped things that float as you can.

6 *They contain air.*
Find some solid objects with no air in them that float.

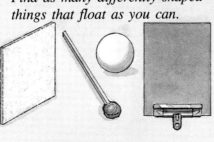

Find some objects containing air that sink.

Looking at results

- *What is the same about all the things that float?*
- *What is the same about all the things that sink?*

National Curriculum

...investigate the factors involved in floating and sinking.

Shopping bags

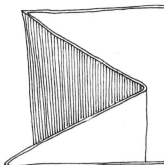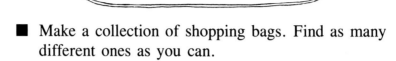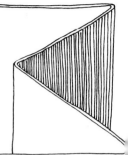

■ Make a collection of shopping bags. Find as many different ones as you can.

■ Fill in this observation sheet.

Bag number	Shop	Made of	Designed to carry	Shape of handle
1				
2				
3				
4				
5				
6				
7				
8				
9				
10				

■ Is there a connection between the shape of the handle and the things carried in the bag?

Shopping bags

▼▼▼▼▼▼▼▼▼▼▼▼▼▼▼▼▼▼▼▼▼▼▼▼▼▼▼▼

Attainment Target
Physical processes
Themes
Shopping, Food,
Forces, Transport

Asking questions

Which kind of handle is the strongest for a shopping bag?

It might be that ...

*A circle cut in the bag is the best.
A semicircular handle, glued on, is the best.*

Experimenting

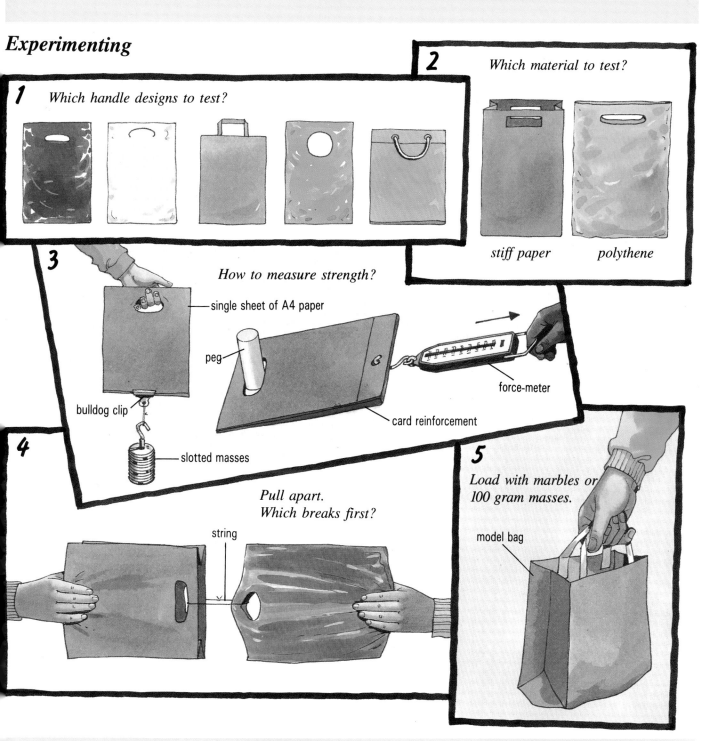

1 *Which handle designs to test?*

2 *Which material to test?*

stiff paper   polythene

3 *How to measure strength?*

- single sheet of A4 paper
- peg
- force-meter
- bulldog clip
- card reinforcement
- slotted masses

4 *Pull apart. Which breaks first?*

string

5 *Load with marbles or 100 gram masses.*

model bag

Looking at results

- *How many times can each handle be tested?*
- *Where does each handle begin to give way? Can improvements be made on the basis of this observation?*

Variables to keep the same (frame 1)

- *Material used (A4 writing paper)*
- *Amount of paper used*
- *Way in which strength is measured*

Variable to change

- *Shape of handle*

National Curriculum

*...experience the natural force of gravity pulling things down
...investigate the strength of a simple structure*

Through the air

▼▼▼▼▼▼▼▼▼▼▼▼▼▼▼▼▼▼▼▼▼▼▼▼

People who play ball games often want to throw or kick
the ball as far as possible. Investigate how they do it.

■ Make a catapult for a paper ball.

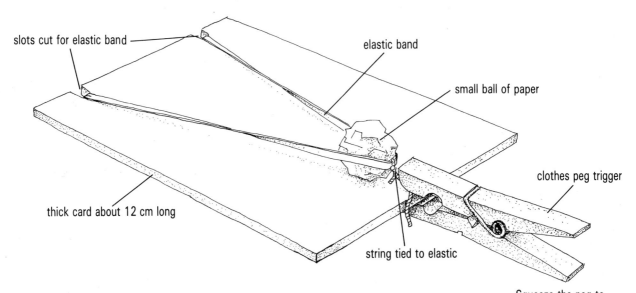

slots cut for elastic band

elastic band

small ball of paper

clothes peg trigger

thick card about 12 cm long

string tied to elastic

Squeeze the peg to
release the catapult

■ Pull the elastic back to different positions and see how
far the ball goes for each position.

▲ TAKE CARE! Do not aim the ball in anyone's
direction.

■ Try different elastic bands.

■ Try different sizes of paper ball.

Through the air

▼ ▼

Attainment Target
Physical processes
Themes
Sport, Weapons,
Toys and games,
Moving things

Asking questions

Which is the best angle at which to throw a ball so that it goes as far as possible?

It might be that ...

A large angle (60°) is the best.

Experimenting

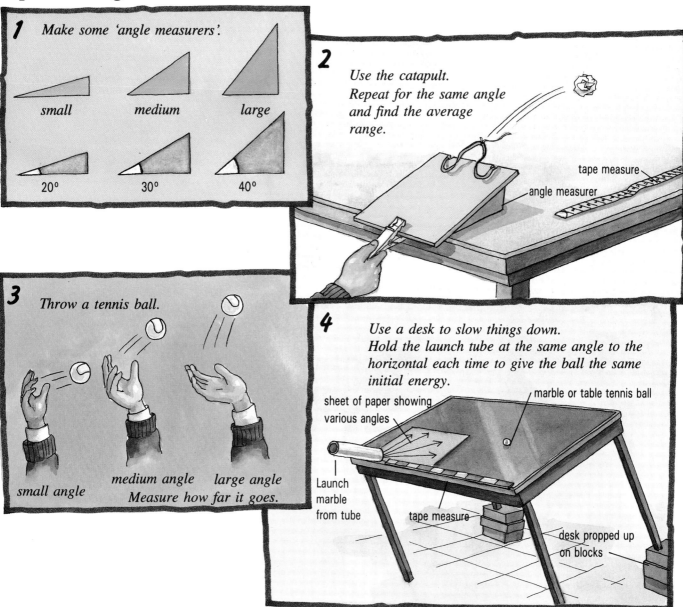

1 *Make some 'angle measurers'.*

small   medium   large

20°   30°   40°

2 *Use the catapult. Repeat for the same angle and find the average range.*

tape measure
angle measurer

3 *Throw a tennis ball.*

small angle   medium angle   large angle
Measure how far it goes.

4 *Use a desk to slow things down. Hold the launch tube at the same angle to the horizontal each time to give the ball the same initial energy.*

sheet of paper showing various angles
marble or table tennis ball
Launch marble from tube
tape measure
desk propped up on blocks

Looking at results

● *Plotting the results*

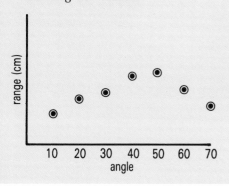

● *If the results are plotted on a scatter graph, they should show an optimum angle of about 45° for the greatest range.*
● *Use a computer spreadsheet or database to help.*

Variables to keep the same

● *The ball*
● *The energy of projection*

Variable to change

● *Angle of projection*

National Curriculum

... early experience of devices which move ...forces should be experienced in the way they push, pull, make things move ...explore different types of forces ...and use measurements to compare their effects in, for example, moving things

79

Colour dots

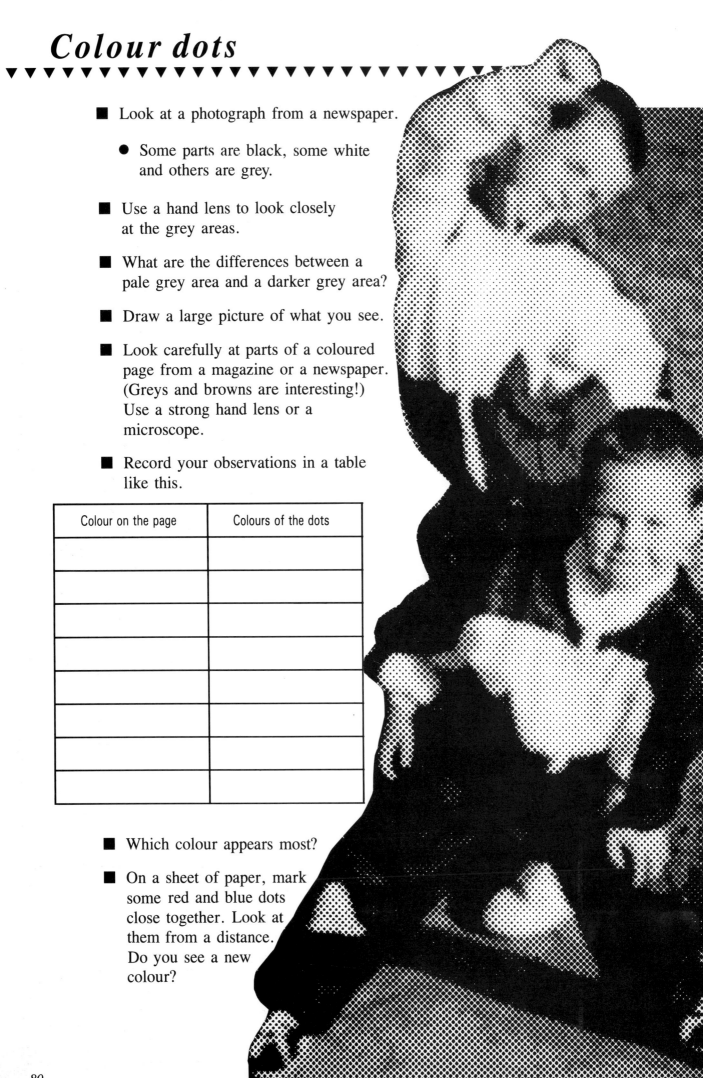

■ Look at a photograph from a newspaper.

  ● Some parts are black, some white
    and others are grey.

■ Use a hand lens to look closely
  at the grey areas.

■ What are the differences between a
  pale grey area and a darker grey area?

■ Draw a large picture of what you see.

■ Look carefully at parts of a coloured
  page from a magazine or a newspaper.
  (Greys and browns are interesting!)
  Use a strong hand lens or a
  microscope.

■ Record your observations in a table
  like this.

Colour on the page	Colours of the dots

■ Which colour appears most?

■ On a sheet of paper, mark
  some red and blue dots
  close together. Look at
  them from a distance.
  Do you see a new
  colour?

Colour dots

▼▼▼▼▼▼▼▼▼▼▼▼▼▼▼▼▼▼▼▼▼▼▼▼▼▼▼▼

Attainment Target
Physical processes
Themes
Light and colour,
Newspapers and
magazines,
Photography,
Ourselves

Asking questions

Which is the best way to see a
brown from a distance using
different coloured marks?

It might be that ...

Mixing red and green dots is best.
Mixing dashes of yellow, red and
blue is best.
Mixing squares of red and blue is
best.

Experimenting

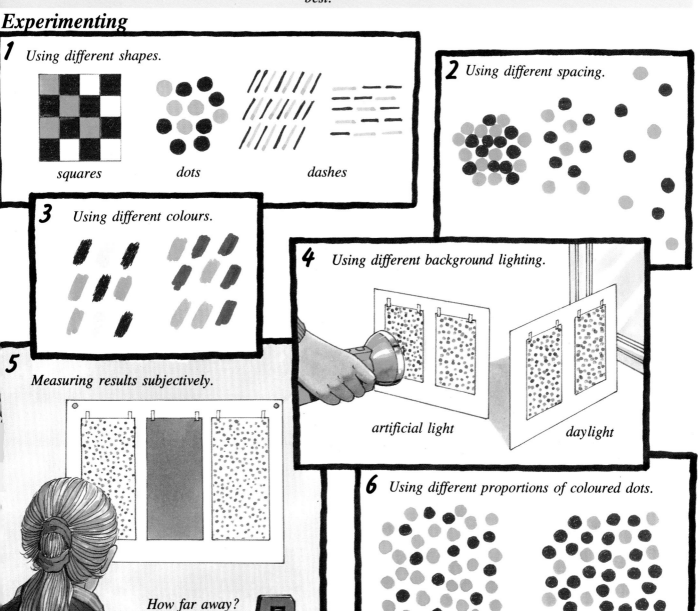

1 Using different shapes.

squares   dots   dashes

2 Using different spacing.

3 Using different colours.

4 Using different background lighting.

artificial light   daylight

5 Measuring results subjectively.

How far away?

6 Using different proportions of coloured dots.

Looking at results

- Is blue + orange the same
  effect as blue + red + yellow?
- What is the relationship
  between size of mark and
  best viewing distance?

Variables to keep the same (frame 2)

- Colours
- Shape marks
- Lighting
- Look from same distance

Variable to change

- Spaces between dots

National Curriculum

...explore light sources and the
effects related to ...colour
...represent ...their ideas about
how light varies in terms of
...colour

Paper glider

▼▼▼▼▼▼▼▼▼▼▼▼▼▼▼▼▼▼▼▼▼▼▼▼▼

■ Make a simple paper glider.

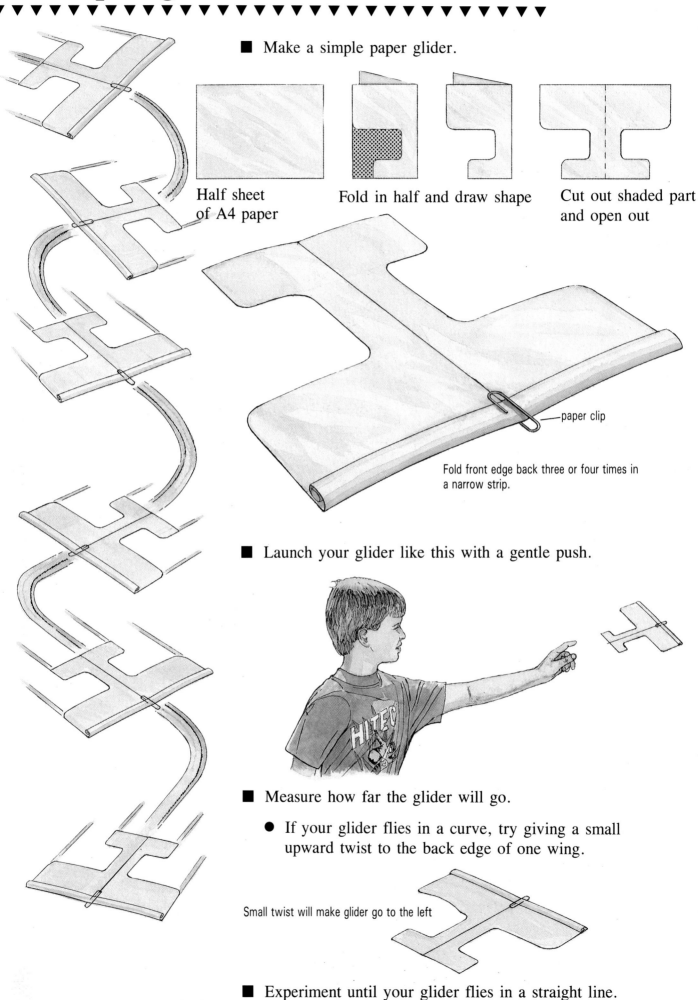

Half sheet
of A4 paper

Fold in half and draw shape

Cut out shaded part
and open out

——paper clip

Fold front edge back three or four times in
a narrow strip.

■ Launch your glider like this with a gentle push.

■ Measure how far the glider will go.

● If your glider flies in a curve, try giving a small
upward twist to the back edge of one wing.

Small twist will make glider go to the left

■ Experiment until your glider flies in a straight line.

Paper glider

▼▼▼▼▼▼▼▼▼▼▼▼▼▼▼▼▼▼▼▼▼▼

Attainment Targets
Physical processes,
Materials and their
properties
Themes
Flight, Transport,
Toys and games, Air,
Moving things

Asking questions	It might be that ...
How can I make the glider fly further?	*Making it with tissue paper will help.*
	Making wider wings will help.
What will happen if I change the size of the glider?	*It will tend to nose dive.*
What will happen if I glue on a rudder?	*It will be easier to steer and get a longer flight.*

Experimenting *What will happen if I change the size of the glider?*

1 *Keep the paper to the same proportions.*

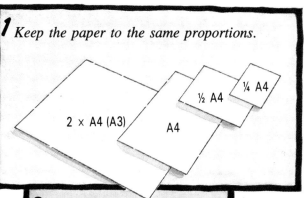

2 × A4 (A3)   A4   ½ A4   ¼ A4

2

Fly each glider in the same way two or three times.

tape measure

3 *Try changing the proportions of the glider.*

longer and narrower

OR

shorter and wider

4 *Try using different materials.*

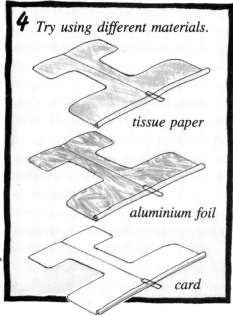

tissue paper

aluminium foil

card

5 *Where is the best place to fix a rudder for better steering?*

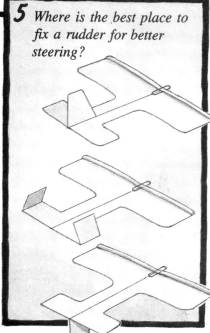

Looking at results

GLIDER	length	width	distance flown 1 2 3	average
A				

RESULTS

- Does the glider fly further the bigger it gets?
- Is there an optimum size?
- Can you predict the best size from the data you have?

distance flown (cm)

length of glider (cm)

Variables to keep the same (frame 4)

- Size of glider
- Shape of glider
- Nose weight

Variable to change

- *Material of which the glider is made*

National Curriculum

...experience of devices which move ...explore different types of forces including gravity and use measurements to compare their effects in, for example, moving things

Magnetic attraction

▼▼▼▼▼▼▼▼▼▼▼▼▼▼▼▼▼▼▼▼▼▼▼▼▼▼▼▼

■ Collect some different magnets.

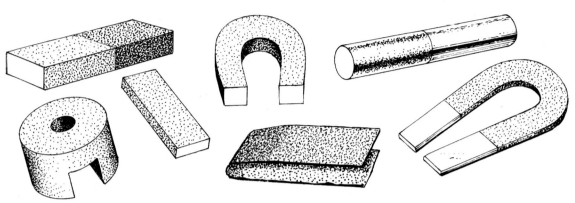

■ Put them near some different materials.

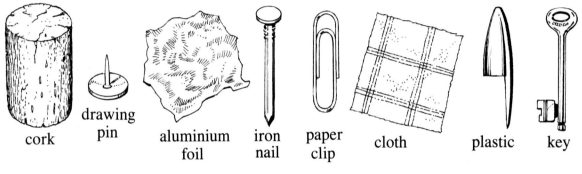

cork   drawing pin   aluminium foil   iron nail   paper clip   cloth   plastic   key

■ Make a list of the things that 'stick' to the magnets.

Things that stick to a magnet

Paper clip

drawing pin

■ What do the things on your list have in common?

■ Find out if the pull of a magnet can work through other materials.

through air

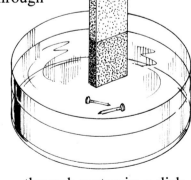

through water in a dish

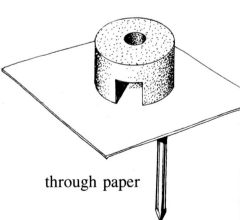

through paper

■ Try some other materials between the magnet and the paper clip.

aluminium foil   thin balsa wood   plastic   polystyrene

■ Record your results.

Magnetic attraction

▼ ▼

Attainment Target
Physical processes
Themes
Magnets, Forces,
Toys and games,
Moving things

Asking questions

Which magnet has the strongest pull?

Is the pull of a magnet equal at both ends (poles)?

Are the heavier magnets the stronger ones?

It might be that ...

The horse shoe magnet is the strongest.

The pull is stronger at the north pole of the magnet.

The heavier magnets are the stronger.

Experimenting *Which magnet has the strongest pull?*

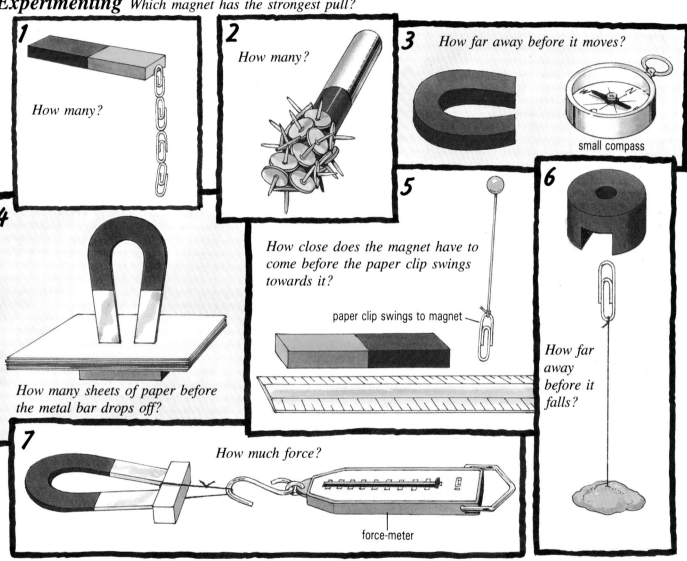

1. How many?

2. How many?

3. How far away before it moves? small compass

4. How many sheets of paper before the metal bar drops off?

5. How close does the magnet have to come before the paper clip swings towards it? paper clip swings to magnet

6. How far away before it falls?

7. How much force? force-meter

Looking at results

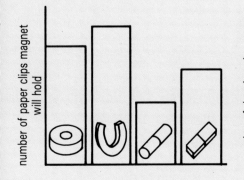

number of paper clips magnet will hold

number of drawing pins magnet will hold

heavy and strong

weight of magnet (grams)

Is there a correlation?

Variables to keep the same (frame 5)

- *Size of paper clip*
- *Length of thread*
- *Speed of approach of magnet*

Variable to change

- *The magnet*

National Curriculum

...explore the effect of magnets on a variety of magnetic and non-magnetic materials

Slippery surfaces

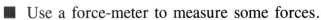

Friction is a force that tries to stop or slow down movement.

■ Use a force-meter to measure some forces.

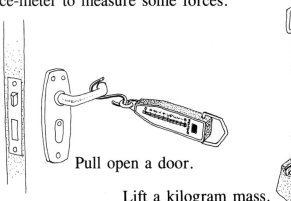

Pull open a door.

Lift a kilogram mass.

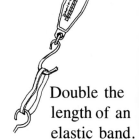

force-meter measuring to 10 newtons

Double the length of an elastic band.

■ Measure the friction force between two surfaces.
  ● Record your results.

*The friction force is the **same** as the pulling force when the block is moving smoothly.*

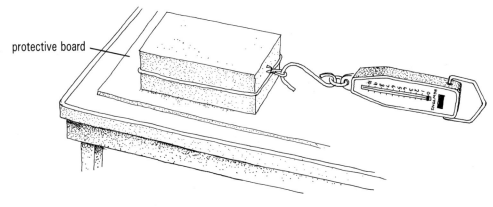

protective board

  ● Measure the force when the block is moving smoothly

■ Do this a few times. Do you always get the same result?

■ Put something slippery, such as cooking oil, between the block and the board. Measure the friction force again.
  ● Record your results

*The slippery substance is called a **lubricant**.*

Try putting different lubricants like these on your han and feel how slippery they are. Write them down in order of slipperiness.
  ● cooking oil   ● bicycle oil
  ● talcum powder   ● margarine
  ● petroleum jelly   ● soap and water

Slippery surfaces

▼▼▼▼▼▼▼▼▼▼▼▼▼▼▼▼▼▼▼▼▼▼▼

Attainment Targets
Physical processes,
Materials and their
properties
Themes
Moving things,
Transport, Homes

Asking questions

Which is the best lubricant?

Does the temperature affect a lubricant?

It might be that ...

Soapy water is the best lubricant.

It makes some lubricants work better.

Experimenting *Which is the best lubricant?*

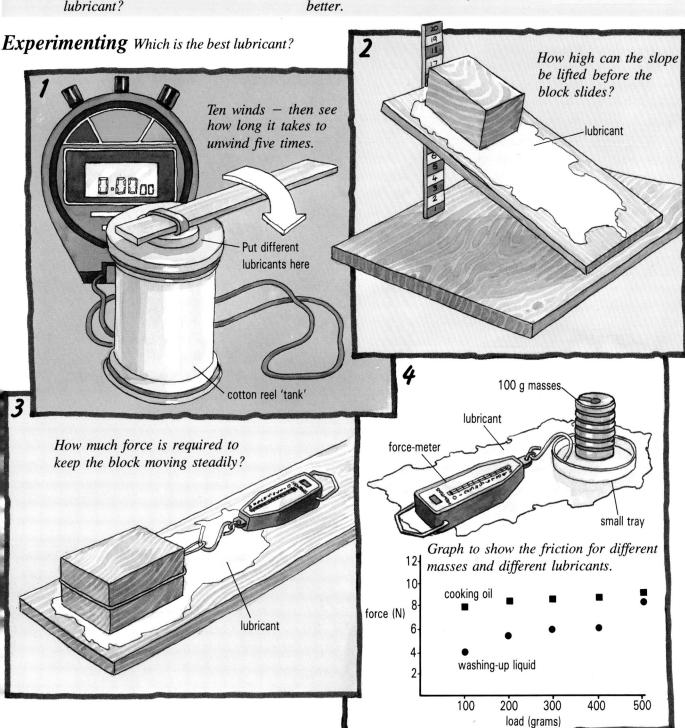

1

Ten winds — then see how long it takes to unwind five times.

Put different lubricants here

cotton reel 'tank'

2

How high can the slope be lifted before the block slides?

lubricant

3

How much force is required to keep the block moving steadily?

lubricant

4

100 g masses

lubricant

force-meter

small tray

Graph to show the friction for different masses and different lubricants.

cooking oil

washing-up liquid

force (N)

load (grams)

Looking at results

- *Is the friction force consistent?*
- *Does the mass of the pulled object make a difference?*
- *What do the best lubricants have in common?*

Variables to keep the same (frame 2)

- *Same block of wood*
- *Same surface*
- *Same amount of lubricant on surface*
- *Same rate at which slope is raised*

Variable to change

- *Type of lubricant*

National Curriculum

...forces should be experienced in the way they push, pull, make things move ...explore friction

Paper springs

▼▼▼▼▼▼▼▼▼▼▼▼▼▼▼▼▼▼▼▼▼▼▼▼▼▼▼

■ Make a paper spring.

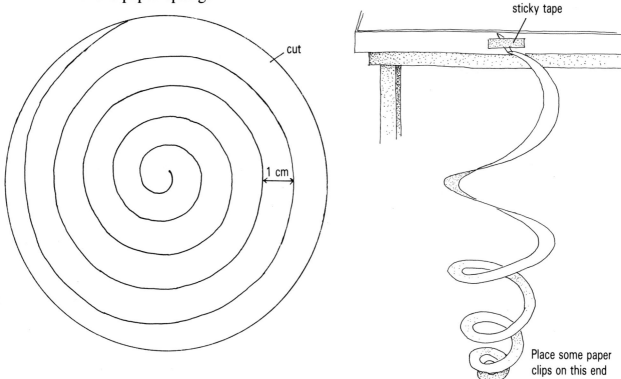

■ Hang the spring up with some sticky tape.

■ Complete this table of information for your spring.

Number of paper clips	Distance spring hangs down (cm)
1	
2	
3	
4	
5	
6	
7	
8	
9	
10	

■ Draw a simple graph to show your results.

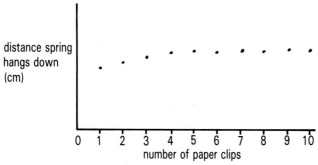

■ Can you predict what will happen if you hang on another paper clip?

88

Paper springs

▼▼▼▼▼▼▼▼▼▼▼▼▼▼▼▼▼▼▼▼▼▼▼▼▼▼▼

Attainment Targets
Physical processes,
Materials and their
properties
Themes
Forces, Paper,
Shape, Machines

Asking questions

*What kind of graph pattern will I
get using other spring materials?*

*What difference will different
spring shapes make to their
springiness?*

It might be that ...

*Newspaper may stretch further to
begin with to give a curved graph.
Polythene has no springiness.*

*A square spring will not be as
springy as a circle.*

Experimenting

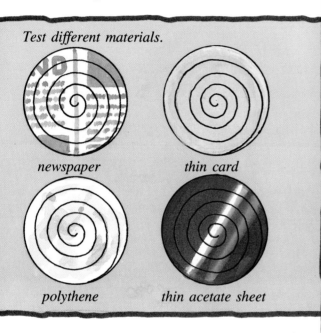

1 Test different materials.

newspaper   thin card

polythene   thin acetate sheet

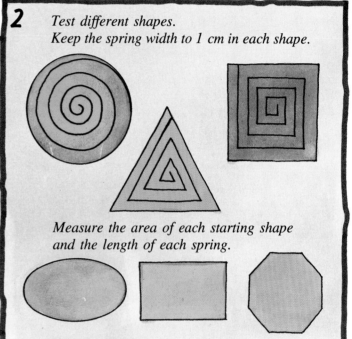

2 Test different shapes.
Keep the spring width to 1 cm in each shape.

Measure the area of each starting shape
and the length of each spring.

Looking at results (frame 1)

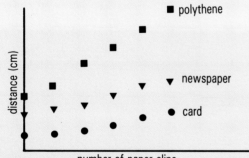

■ polythene

distance (cm)

▼ newspaper

● card

number of paper clips

- *How do the materials compare?*
- *Why are there differences?*

Variables to keep the same

- *Starting shape, eg circle*
- *Size of starting shape*
- *Width of spring, eg 1 cm*
- *Method of loading, eg paper clips*

Variable to change

- *Springy material*

Looking at results (frame 2)

- *Is there a correlation between the length of
the spring and the distance stretched under,
say, five paper clips?*

Variables to keep the same

- *Type of material*
- *Width of spring*
- *Method of loading*
- *Area of starting shape*

Variable to change

- *Starting shape of spring*

National Curriculum

*...forces should be experienced in the way they
pull ...and change the shape of objects*

String telephone

▼▼▼▼▼▼▼▼▼▼▼▼▼▼▼▼▼▼▼▼▼▼▼▼▼▼▼

■ Make the string telephone and test it.

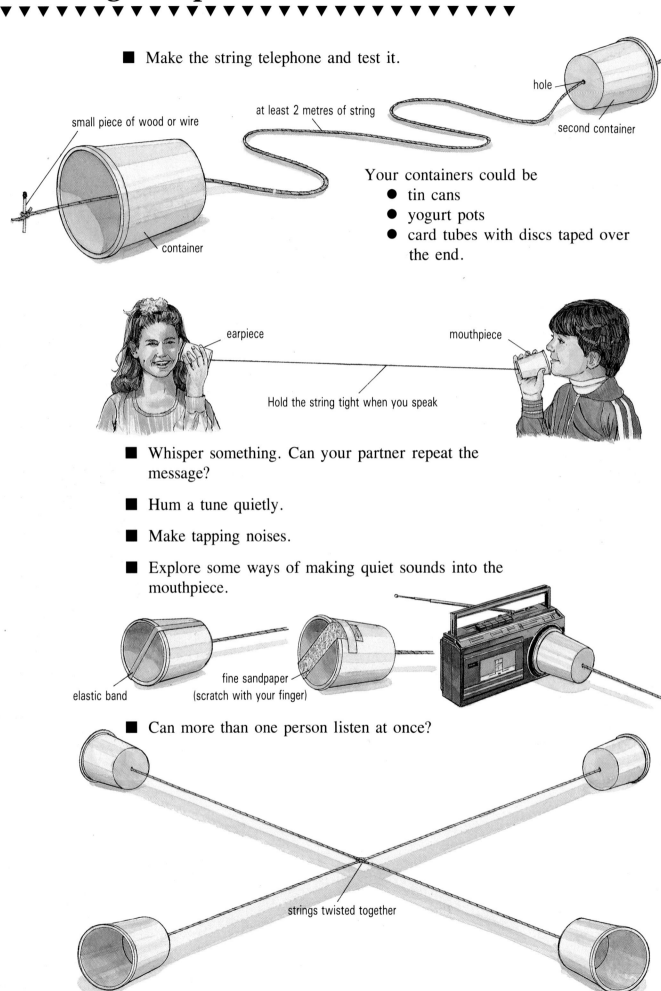

hole

second container

small piece of wood or wire

at least 2 metres of string

container

Your containers could be
- tin cans
- yogurt pots
- card tubes with discs taped over the end.

earpiece

mouthpiece

Hold the string tight when you speak

■ Whisper something. Can your partner repeat the message?

■ Hum a tune quietly.

■ Make tapping noises.

■ Explore some ways of making quiet sounds into the mouthpiece.

elastic band

fine sandpaper
(scratch with your finger)

■ Can more than one person listen at once?

strings twisted together

String telephone

Attainment Target
Physical processes
Themes
Sound,
Communications,
Helping others,
Toys and games

Asking questions

Which is the best material for the 'string'?

Which container makes the best mouthpiece?

How long can the string be and a soft sound still heard?

It might be that ...

Cotton thread is best.

A plastic film canister is best.

The length of the playground is possible.

Experimenting Which is the best material for the 'string'?

1 Which 'strings'?

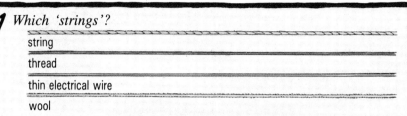

string

thread

thin electrical wire

wool

2

sound sensor connected to a computer data-logger

Measuring objectively.

3 Measuring the 'best' telephone subjectively.

4 Increase the volume of sound until it is heard.

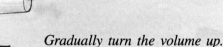

Gradually turn the volume up.

Yes!

5 Keeping the string taut.

6

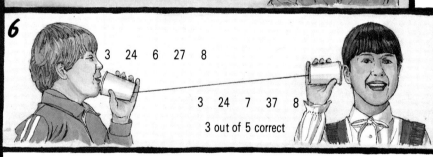

3 24 6 27 8

3 24 7 37 8

3 out of 5 correct

Looking at results

- Compare the shape of computer data-logging graphs.

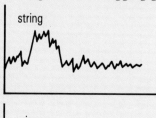

string

wire

- Can you say one string is twice as good as another?
- Do other groups get similar results?
- Are the results consistent?

Variables to keep the same

- Mouthpiece
- Earpiece
- Length of 'string'
- Method of making sounds
- Person receiving sounds
- Tension in 'string'

Variable to change

- Type of 'string'

National Curriculum

...experience the range of sounds in their immediate environment and to find out about their causes and uses ...learn that sounds are heard because they travel to the ear and thay they can do so via a variety of materials ...should learn that sounds are made when objects vibrate

Building walls

■ Find some things with which to build 'walls'. You will need lots of 'bricks' the same size.

Try: coins lolly sticks cubes rods

wooden blocks card boxes

■ Find different ways of building walls.

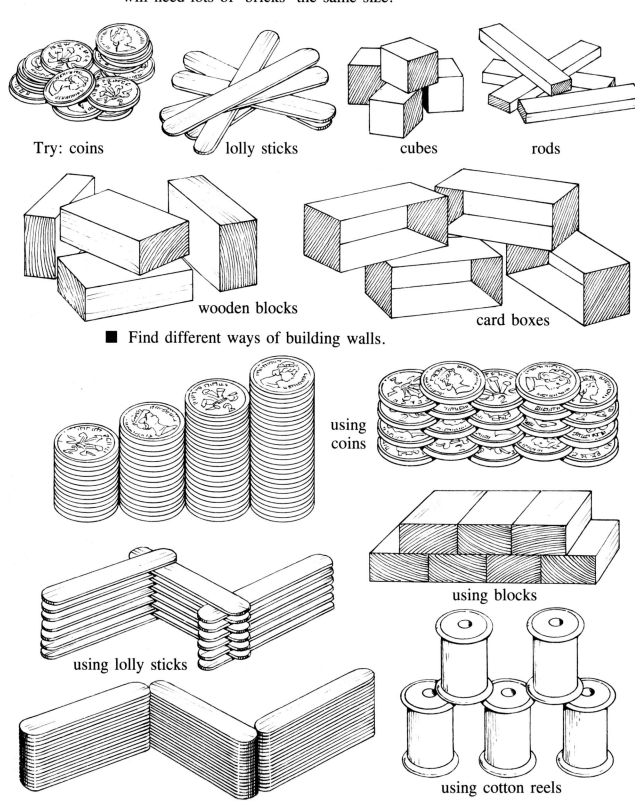

using coins

using blocks

using lolly sticks

using cotton reels

Building walls

▼▼▼▼▼▼▼▼▼▼▼▼▼▼▼▼▼▼▼▼▼▼▼▼

Attainment Target
Physical processes
Themes
Homes, Buildings,
Forces

Asking questions

Which way of making a wall is the strongest?

Which wall will stand up to a strong wind?

It might be that ...

A wall with overlapping bricks is the strongest.

A wall with holes in stands up best to a wind.

Experimenting *Which way of making a wall is the strongest?*

1 Shake the table. Which wall falls first?

2 Make an 'earthquake'. Pull out suddenly. How many 'earthquakes' before the wall falls?

3 Blow hard. How hard was the blow?

4 Use a fan to make a wind. How many waves of the fan?

5

6 How far out should it be pulled?

plastic coins

table tennis ball

Looking at results

- *Draw the best pattern of bricks each time.*
- *Is it always the same kind of pattern which is best?*
- *How could you describe this pattern?*

Variables to keep the same

- *Method of knocking the wall down*
- *Type of 'brick' used*
- *Number of bricks*

Variable to change

- *The way the wall is made*

National Curriculum

...forces should be experienced in the way they push, pull, make things move ... investigate the strength of a simple structure

Which ball?

▼▼▼▼▼▼▼▼▼▼▼▼▼▼▼▼▼▼▼▼▼▼▼▼▼▼

■ Collect a number of different balls.

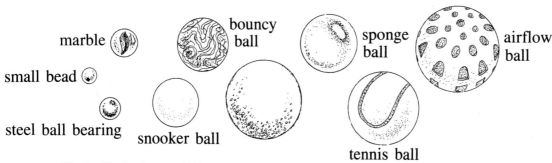

marble
bouncy ball
sponge ball
airflow ball
small bead
steel ball bearing
snooker ball
tennis ball

■ Roll them on different surfaces.

carpet   linoleum   playground   wooden desk top

● Do they each roll differently?
● Try to work out why.

Racing down a slope

■ Roll two balls down a slope and along a level surface.

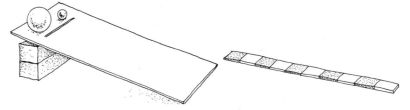

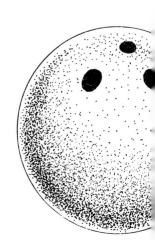

■ Measure how far each ball rolls on the level surface.

■ Take another two balls and predict which one will roll
  the further. Roll them down the slope from the same
  spot and see if you were right.

■ Do this again for some other pairs of balls.

■ Fill in a table like this
  one for your results. Write
  the winners in the spaces.

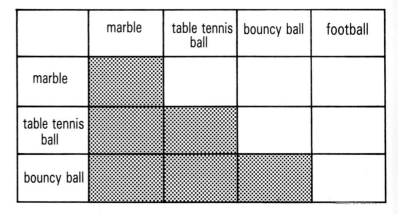

	marble	table tennis ball	bouncy ball	football
marble				
table tennis ball				
bouncy ball				

Which ball?

▼▼▼▼▼▼▼▼▼▼▼▼▼▼▼▼▼▼▼▼▼▼▼

Attainment Target
Physical processes
Themes
Moving things,
Energy, Toys and
games, Sport

Asking questions

*What makes a ball roll further
along a surface?*

*What difference does the level
surface make to the distance a ball
rolls?*

It might be that ...

*It is the colour of the ball.
It is the weight of the ball.
It is the diameter of the ball.
It is the material the ball is
made from.*

*The ball rolls further on a hard
surface.
The ball rolls further on a
smooth surface*

Experimenting *What makes a ball roll further on a carpet?*

1 It is the diameter of the ball. — largest diameter — smallest diameter

2

Test for all balls on carpet		
Ball	Diameter	Distance rolled
Marble	1·3 cm	54 cm
Football		
Table		

3 Test all balls on a variety of surfaces.

4

Slope height: 30 cm

Ball	Material	Diameter	Mass	Surface	Distance rolled
Football	leather	26 cm			
Steel ball					

Looking at results

*For all balls on a variety of
surfaces:*

- *Use a computer database to
  record the results.*
- *Use the database to isolate
  results, such as those for
  carpet only (use Search).
  Analyse these results
  separately.*
- *Use the database to plot a
  scattergraph for distance
  rolled and mass of ball OR
  distance rolled and diameter
  of ball.*
- *Look for correlations in the
  results.*

diameter (cm) / distance rolled (cm)

*This scattergraph shows a trend:
the larger the diameter, the
further the ball rolls.*

Variables to keep the same (frame 1)

- *Height of slope*

- *Point at which ball is
  released*
- *Surface on which ball rolls*
- *Method of release at the top
  of the slope*

Variable to change

- *Diameter of the ball*

National Curriculum

*experience of devices which
move ...explore different types of
forces including gravity and use
measurements to compare their
effects in, for example, moving
things*